Beyond the Track by Anna Ford is breakthrough racehorse literature, concisely covering every facet of what to expect and how to get the most out of your off-the-track Thoroughbred (OTTB), both mentally and physically. The book could also be called 'OTTB Training for Dummies' or 'OTTB Training A–Z.' I consider this book the ultimate in training manuals for anyone thinking about adopting an ex-racehorse. Anna Ford is uniquely qualified to be the author of this book, which reads easily and covers every important detail of transitioning a horse from the racetrack to his next career."

—LIZ HARRIS, EXECUTIVE DIRECTOR
Thoroughbred Charities of America
To provide a better life for Thoroughbreds, both during and after their racing careers by supporting retirement, rescue, and research, and by helping the people who work with them.

"I'm a strong supporter of finding good homes for Thoroughbreds once they retire from the racetrack. I think it is great that Anna Ford has put together a book to help assist in the training process. These horses are great athletes and definitely can go on to be successful in new careers with the proper guidance and training. I believe Anna is a special person—through her work and dedication she has made it possible for these Thoroughbreds to have a second chance at life."

—NICK ZITO, THOROUGHBRED TRAINER
National Museum of Racing Hall of Fame Inductee

"A great book where very loving, caring people teach others how to share love with a horse, give him new opportunities, and bring out the best in both horse and rider. It is necessary to learn to handle Thoroughbreds the right way, and the author does a great job explaining detail."

—EDGAR PRADO, JOCKEY
Winner of over 6,000 races and the 2006 Eclipse Award, and 2008 National Museum of Racing Hall of Fame Nominee

Beyond the Track

Retraining the Thoroughbred from Racehorse to Riding Horse

ANNA MORGAN FORD

with Amber Heintzberger

Foreword by KAREN O'CONNOR
Olympic Medalist in Eventing

TRAFALGAR SQUARE
North Pomfret, Vermont

First published in 2008 by
Trafalgar Square Books
North Pomfret, Vermont 05053

Printed in China

Library of Congress Cataloging-in-Publication Data

Ford, Anna Morgan.
  Beyond the track : retraining the thoroughbred--from racehorse to riding horse / Anna Morgan Ford ; with Amber Heintzberger.
    p. cm.
  Includes bibliographical references.
  ISBN 978-1-57076-402-8 (alk. paper)
  1. Thoroughbred horse--Training. I. Heintzberger, Amber. II. Title.
  SF293.T5F67 2008
        636.1'32--dc22
                        2007048823

Photo credits:
Jennay Hitesman (pp. iv, 32, 42, 45–6, 48, 57 *top*, 71 *bottom*, 80, 81 *top*, 86, 105 *left*, 134, 137 *left*, 160–1, 169, 207, 218, 220); Emily Lang (pp. xii, 12, 15 *top*, 22 *middle*, 23, 28, 139, 156); Jason Stewart (p. 4); Jim Miller (p. 6); Julie Caldwell (pp. 7 *bottom*, 8, 34, 53–5, 57 *bottom*, 62–3, 66, 71 *top*, 94, 98–9, 103, 108, 114, 116, 118–9, 122, 124, 126–9, 131–2, 137 *right*, 140–151, 153–4, 163, 165, 168 *right*, 171, 176, 183–5, 187, 210–1, 213, 215–7); Pat Lang (p. 10 *left*); Amber Heintzberger (pp. 10 *right*, 16 *right*, 17 *right*, 18 *top right, bottom left*, 50 *left*, 83, 92, 95–7, 101–2, 159, 177, 189 *left*, 198, 226, 231, 233, 243); Anna Ford (pp. 7 *top*, 11, 15 *bottom*, 17 *left*, 18 *top left, bottom right*, 41, 50 *right*, 51–2, 56, 70, 72, 76–7, 81 *bottom*, 100, 105 *right*, 112, 164, 166, 172, 178–181, 189 *right*, 190–1, 196–7, 199–201, 204, 219, 221–3); John Engelhardt (pp. 16 *left*, 19, 22 *left, right*, 167, 168 *left*, 174); Bob Tarr (p. 31); Carrie Paston (pp. 37, 136); James Leslie Parker (p. 237); courtesy of Lisa Croxton (p. 235); courtesy of Mary Jo Gehrum (p. 239); courtesy of VW Perry (pp. 228, 241)
Photo 3.5 (p. 49) is from *All Horse Systems Go: The Horse Owner's Full-Color Veterinary Care and Conditioning Reference for Modern Performance, Sport, and Pleasure Horses* by Nancy S. Loving, DVM, and used by permission of the author.
Photo 8.4 C (p. 137 *right*) is from *Complete Holistic Care and Healing for Horses: The Owner's Veterinary Guide to Alternative Methods and Remedies* by Mary Brennan, DVM, and used by permission of the author.

Book design by Carrie Fradkin
Jacket design by Heather Mansfield
Typefaces: Arno Pro, Hypatia Sans Pro

10 9 8 7 6 5 4 3

Dedication

I would like to dedicate this book to the individuals and programs that have devoted time and energy to giving off-the-track Thoroughbreds new careers. It is through such efforts that thousands of once unwanted horses can become desirable with bright, promising futures.

Contents

Foreword by Karen O'Connor

It has been my privilege to ride and compete horses for much of my life. Horses have the ability to teach people wonderful virtues, and I can say, quite honestly, I would have been a very different individual without them. The one thing that always amazes me is the number of things horses can do with their talents at the hands of man. They are an incredibly versatile species.

For centuries, the racing industry has been breeding Thoroughbreds. Breeders have continually improved upon the horse's natural instinct and ability to run. Many studies have been done to develop horses for different distances. With all this attention on the specifics of the well-bred racing machine, other attributes and talents have come through collaterally: with the powerful engine for the gallop also came the ability to jump high and move gracefully, as well as fantastic lung capacity for endurance purposes. And, possibly the most intangible—and valuable—attribute of all, is the great heart and "try" these horses possess.

Horse racing is "as American as apple pie." Racing crosses all barriers. It is a part of our American heritage. Even during the Great Depression, horse racing was an integral part of life and source of financial stability for many. The phrase "bet the farm" had true meaning at that time, and all hopes would hinge on a special horse bringing it home for a single family and their survival.

With these kinds of pressures on an industry, it is no surprise that the number of horses racing has grown exponentially. There are more racehorses than ever, and there is more talent out there, too.

Most Thoroughbreds have completed their racing careers about the same time others are just getting started. I have been lucky enough to benefit from the talents of many of these horses leaving racing and starting second careers. I know for myself, I always look forward to a phone call from one of my contacts at the track. Stories that begin with, "I can't keep him in the paddock," or "He trots too big for us," are music to my ears. My favorite is always, "This horse is just too laid back—he has a great gallop but doesn't want to be in front." I'll make a lovely sport horse out of that racing shortfall; I'll show this horse that he, too, can be great.

Well-bred Thoroughbred mares play a huge role in our small breeding program, as well. My husband, David, and I have enjoyed lovely progeny from these mares and hope for some real future stars.

It is so refreshing to see *Beyond the Track,* a book that addresses the necessary steps for achieving success with the ex-racehorse. I thank Anna Ford for this fantastic resource and reference, and I hope you enjoy the book as I have.

I look forward to seeing your next superstar off-the-track!

Karen O'Connor
2007 US Equestrian Federation Equestrian of the Year
Ten-Time US Eventing Association Lady Rider of the Year
Winner of Individual and Team Gold Medals, 2007 Pan American Games
Winner of Team Silver and Bronze Medals, 1996 and 2000 Olympic Games
Three-Time Winner of Rolex Kentucky CCI****

Introduction

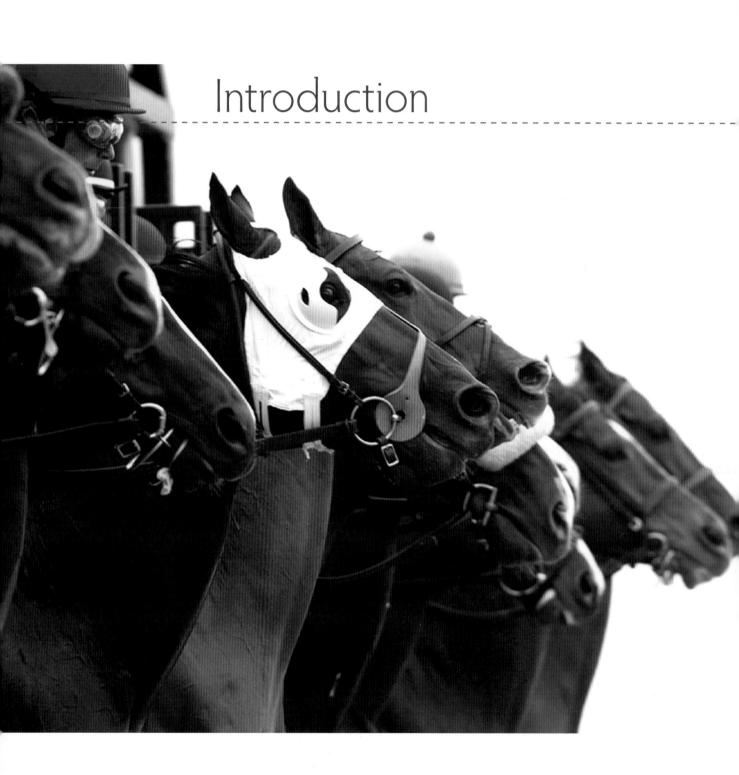

Ever since the first Thoroughbred race was run hundreds of years ago, there has been a need for people to help "transition" retired racehorses into new careers. In a business that rolls a lot of dice in the hopes that one will be a winner, it is natural that many of the horses bred and trained to run will fail to meet expectations—they might be too aggressive or spooky in nature, they might not be fast enough, or they might get hurt early in the game, rendering them unable to reach their racing potential. In North America alone, the Jockey Club registers over 37,000 Thoroughbred foals each year. A third of them might go on to be viable stakes winners or breeding stock. The rest...well, the rest are unsure of their fate.

It was in 1992 that it became apparent to my mother and me that a vast number of off-the-track Thoroughbreds (OTTBs) were in desperate need of new homes, and so we took up the challenge and organized New Vocations Racehorse Adoption. Our focus is to prepare ex-racehorses for new jobs, rather than retire them from all service. There are "retirement farms" where OTTBs are essentially "put out to pasture" for the remainder of their life—a suitable situation for injured animals or those that, for one reason or another, may not be able to perform another job. However, we felt that many OTTBs—with a little time and training—could in fact go on to excel in a different sport, or simply bring joy to a family as a pleasure mount.

As we began offering ex-racehorses a safe haven, rehabilitation from injury, and retraining, we quickly learned that although OTTBs are, in many ways, different from other types of horses, there is great potential in each one of them. Yes, Thoroughbreds are bred to run. But, they are not just "running machines"; they have great hearts, too. Once a Thoroughbred is retrained for riding he will do anything for his rider and handler. Many act like children and constantly seek their owner's approval. Give these guys a job to do, and they will wholeheartedly give it their all!

Through the years I have seen over 1,000 adopted OTTBs leave our program and go to their new homes—New Vocations adopts out more ex-racehorses than any other program in the US. Horses from our program have gone on to become eventers, show ring hunters, jumpers, dressage horses, Pony Club mounts, foxhunters, trail horses, endurance horses, and even barrel racers! Fortunately, most people who take these horses are successful in introducing them to their new lives, though there are inevitably a few who get frustrated and send a horse back to our program.

Over time I have noticed some common factors in the scenarios where OTTBs have been successfully transitioned:

Patience

It can take months—or even years—for a horse to fully work up to a new career. Many of the people who are successful with OTTBs give a horse several months to just relax before they start really working him. Holding a horse to a set time frame only puts unnecessary pressure on both the horse and his owner.

Commitment

An individual who chooses to adopt an animal is taking on, or assuming related responsibilities—often a long list not to be taken lightly! In the case of an OTTB, you are making a commitment to that horse. Doing so often saves the horse's life, since new skills make it less likely the horse will end up in a bad situation, as could happen when he knows little else than how to run fast. There will be good days and bad days, but in order for the horse to find and excel in a new career, the adopter needs to stay fully committed.

Experience

The more experience the adopter has with owning and training horses, the better. OTTBs need a lot of help figuring out how the world works away from the track—from both the ground and the saddle. When they first arrive at New Vocations, they may have bad barn habits, poor ground manners, and can be excitable and strong under saddle. While these are all issues that will likely change with kind and consistent train-

ing, they still require a foundation of horse knowledge and an ability to "read" equine behavior usually gained with experience. Therefore, OTTBs are generally not suitable for first-time horse owners.

Assistance

If an adopter is unable to work through a certain problem with a horse, he or she must be willing to search for someone with experience who can help. In addition, early work with ex-racehorses often requires a second set of hands or a ground person to ensure safety and a positive experience for all involved.

Environment

A safe and welcoming environment where the horse is able to focus on learning his new job is essential. I go into this in more detail later in the book.

Partnership

It takes time to get to know a horse, but by developing a good, working partnership you will have a better understanding of what the horse likes and dislikes. Successful adopters understand the value of working *with* rather than *against* the horse when they encounter a problem, never forcing the horse to mold to a set program. And, sometimes it is necessary to work around a problem—with time and patience—instead of working through it as you might do with other horses.

Overall, I find that success with an

OTTB has a great deal to do with the adopter's mindset. I have seen people who lacked experience, but who were infinitely patient and always willing to ask for help, have more success than others who had plenty of experience but didn't possess the frame of mind to handle an OTTB.

If you decide that you would like to work with an OTTB, you need to realize that you will be in it for the long haul. You must understand that transitioning a Thoroughbred from racetrack to regular life is a challenging experience. You need to roll with the punches, and patiently take the good with the bad.

The purpose of this book is to help you along the way, providing basic information and training tips that will enable the average horseman to prepare the OTTB for a new career. In addition, my recommendations for feeding, farrier work, and socialization are also helpful for transitioning the retiree to simply become a companion or pasture pal.

I will help you deal with everything from your horse's first day at his new home, to his first outing away from home. I'll discuss many of the "peculiarities" of the ex-racehorse, and knowing about these habits and behaviors before you begin retraining will help the process go much more smoothly. This book will not tell you how to train the ex-racehorse to be a hunter, jumper, eventer, or dressage horse, but it will help you build a solid foundation invaluable in the pursuit of any specific discipline.

1 Bred to Run: What Racehorses Know

So you want to bring home a racehorse? You may have seen Thoroughbreds at the track—a blur of color—and felt your heart skip as the horse you picked to win led the field across the finish line. Perhaps you have also seen "transitioned" off-the-track Thoroughbreds (I'll refer to them as "OTTBs" throughout this book) assume their new careers with grace and athleticism and would like to achieve the same success with one yourself . Or, maybe you have heard heartrending stories about the less fortunate "unwanted" racehorses and you feel the need to give one of these a chance at "life."

Every year, literally thousands of racehorses reach the end of their racing career and are available for a new purpose. At New Vocations, we get horses primarily from tracks on the East Coast and in the Midwest. Some Thoroughbred owners donate their horses to our organization when they no longer have a use for them (due to injury, behavior, lack of running ability, or any number of other reasons), and generally because they are unable to find an individual buyer. New horses arrive on a weekly basis, and it isn't unusual to have six delivered in one week.

Upon arrival at New Vocations, each horse is evaluated by the experienced staff. Both mental and physical condition is assessed and a plan to suit the horse's particular needs is devised. The idea is to strategically begin the OTTBs' retraining and enable them to start new careers by evaluating their potential, getting them healthy, handling them safely and patiently, and ultimately placing them in new homes. There are many steps, and each horse moves through them at a different rate. Some immediately relax and grow accustomed to their new life rather quickly, while others take months to fit in.

It isn't until an OTTB is favorably responding to his transitional training that we start looking to place him with a new owner. While we carefully interview prospective adopters and do our best to find suitable matches, people with an interest in adopting a horse often have limited experience with OTTBs specifically. This leads to numerous questions as they work through the transitioning process with their new horse. I will try to provide the answers to these questions, and others, in pages that follow.

Understanding the OTTB

To better imagine what a horse is going through when he leaves the track and starts a new career as a riding horse, try to imagine yourself in a similar situation. Simply put, think about what it would be like to lose the only job that you have ever known and leave all your friends and everything familiar to you. Then, you move to a new town, where you start a job for which you have no training

1.1 A Thoroughbred's breeding and training is planned and carried out with one goal in mind: winning races.

1.2 A–C These three ex-racehorses were adopted through New Vocations and have gone on to excel in new careers. Mill Reef Affair now enjoys eventing with his rider, Jill Cleveland (A). "Tooey" and Kari Briggs are exploring lower level dressage—here they are pictured at Tooey's first show (B). Velvet Cat, shown here in early schooling, is now used for Pony Club (C).

1.3 Many young Thoroughbreds are turned out with their mothers, along with other mares and foals their age. This allows them to gain social skills, strength, and a taste for being competitive.

or prior experience. In this new place, no one speaks your language, the food is nothing you have ever eaten before, and the schedule is entirely different from your usual routine. This is what it is like for a Thoroughbred to leave life at the track and go on to a new career—he is completely out of his comfort zone.

It helps if the person adopting an ex-race-horse—in this case, you—knows something about the horse's previous experiences as you assist him in the transition to his new lifestyle. Getting to know your new horse is like getting to know a new friend—you want to find out about his personality, background, and what makes him tick. It will take a little time together before you understand his personality, his likes and dislikes, but he will never be able to sit down with you over coffee and share the story of his past. Luckily, many Thoroughbred breeding facilities and racing stables are managed somewhat similarly, so you can better understand your OTTB's background by learning a little about racing as a whole. While by no means a thorough lesson in what is a complex industry with many layers and traditions, I will provide a glimpse of what happens off, and on the track, explaining what most Thoroughbreds likely experience at each stage of their race training.

The Younger Years

Even before conception, a Thoroughbred foal's "life" involves a great deal of pedigree research to ensure that a competitive athlete is produced. Breeders accomplish this by studying race records and characteristics of different bloodlines, and then they consider affordability. With Thoroughbred stud fees ranging from $500 to $500,000, producing a foal can be a huge investment even before you consider veterinary fees, managing the broodmare before and after birth, and myriad other expenses to follow.

While people who breed riding horses may focus on producing offspring with good "minds" or outstanding movement, Thoroughbred breeders focus first and foremost on developing strong, fast offspring. The be-all and end-all goal is to have a competitive horse that can win. Of course, not all Thoroughbreds are winners, but one thing is certain—they *all* know how to run. Just watch a new crop of foals in the field sometime—at a very young age, they just naturally race each other. I remember the farrier at New Vocations saying he could *always* pick out the horses destined for success as yearlings—they were always the fastest ones racing around the field. Future winners are the horses that refuse to be beaten, and this can be seen at a very early age, at play.

Thoroughbred racing is a huge, diverse industry with numerous participants at different levels. For example, within the breeding element exist large *commercial* breeding farms that may have over 50 broodmares. These farms breed with the specific purpose of selling stock at Thoroughbred Sales, most commonly, Yearling Sales. And, there are thousands of smaller, *privately owned* farms that breed horses with the intent to race them. Management varies, but in general, most breeding farms take excellent care of both mares and foals. With so much research and money invested in producing each animal, foals get the best of care so they can grow into strong and competitive individuals.

Some farms employ people who devote time each day to handling new foals and familiarizing them with human contact, beginning at birth. Other farms are limited as to how much time they have to spend with each baby. I find those that are handled at a young and impressionable age usually grow into more tractable adult horses.

One thing that most farms generally have in common is that multiple mares and foals are turned out together in large pastures so the foals become socialized with others their age. This allows them to run freely as they develop physically and mentally in a relaxed and natural setting. While indeed an idyllic start to life, all of these youngsters are headed toward the track—either via the sales ring or the farm's own racing string.

Prepping for Sale

In the racing industry, there are, in fact, many different paths that a foal's life may take. As I

A

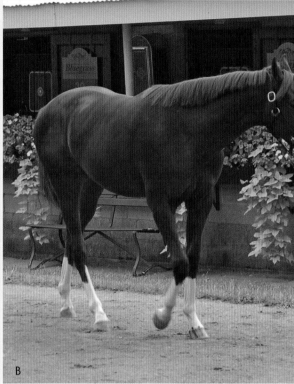

B

1.4 A–E Many Thoroughbreds are specially prepared for sale. Here, a well-behaved weanling is paraded at a Fall Sale (A). Yearlings are conditioned and polished from head-to-toe (B).

mentioned earlier, owners may raise their own foals to race (see p. 14) or to be "prepped for sales." This can be as a foal (with their dam), or in Fall Sales as a weanling, yearling, or as a two-year-old in training.

Weanlings
If the foal is being prepped to sell in the fall as a weanling, chances are the colt or filly will be handled regularly at a young age in order to be ready for the sale. Breeders aim to have their weanlings in top condition, so they are groomed and hand-walked daily, and bathed often. In addition, they are taught to have their feet handled and to stand quietly while their hooves are trimmed.

At the sale, buyers weight conformation and pedigree most heavily.

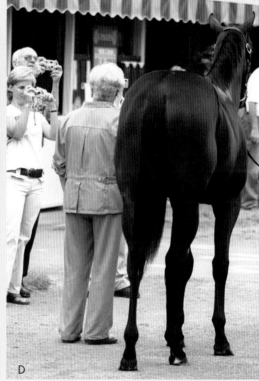

They are expected to stand quietly while inspected by potential buyers (C & D).

Yearlings

If a youngster is not sold as a weanling, or if he shows promise of earning a higher price as a yearling, the owner may hold on to him for a longer stretch of time. Pedigree characteristics aside, yearlings tend to bring higher prices than weanlings because they are closer to racing age and buyers have a better idea of how the horse's body type and conformation will develop.

Prepping yearlings takes anywhere from 60 to 90 days, during which a strict routine conditions them physically and mentally for the sale. Appearance is of utmost importance, so yearlings are kept inside during the hottest part of the day. This helps keep their coats glossy and prevents heat-related stress, which might cause weight loss. Most are groomed daily and participate in a light

For Two-Year-Old Sales, horses are prepared months ahead for a timed two-furlong gallop (E)

exercise program that generally includes hand-walking or slow work on an exercise machine, four or five days a week.

A lot of groundwork is done to teach the yearlings to have good manners and to be comfortable with being led, touched, and having their feet picked up. Their feet are routinely trimmed and painted with hoof conditioner, and some yearlings are even shod for the sale if their feet start to chip or crack.

Over the course of a sale, yearlings are put on display again and again for potential buyers to look them over. (Sales can last days or weeks; however, individual horses are generally only at the sale for two to three days as they are rotated in and out.) They must stand still while their conformation is examined, then willingly and correctly walk, and sometimes trot, along a straight line to show off their movement.

While this sounds simple, there are many distractions for the youngster to contend with. Sales barns are full of activity, and the final—and most intimidating—situation is when the youngster has to stand in the fishbowl-like environment of the sales ring in front of hundreds of people in the audience and a noisy auctioneer. Time is well spent preparing the horse for such a situation with plenty of groundwork and an opportunity to learn to trust his handler.

After the sales, some yearlings go straight into training in their new facilities, while others are given several months of turnout before they are prepared to begin their racing careers.

Two-Year-Olds

Thoroughbreds may also be prepped for the "Two-Year-Old-in-Training" Sales, where not only conformation and pedigree are taken into account but also performance. At these sales, potential buyers may arrive several days early to see each horse gallop a timed two furlongs on the track; the faster the horse, the higher the likely purchase price.

As with those prepped for Yearling Sales, two-year-olds-in-training are also stabled, groomed, and exercised daily for several months prior to the sale. However, these horses have to develop mental toughness early and be able to handle stress well—above and beyond that required of yearlings. So, those intended for Two-Year-Old-in-Training Sales are usually also broke to saddle at the end of their yearling year—in the fall or the winter—as the first sales of the season start as early as February.

When you are researching prospective OTTBs' backgrounds, it may be desirable to consider one that went through the Two-Year-Old-in-Training sales because many of these horses tend to be easier to handle and teach new skills. But, bear in mind the possible negative side effects to this fast-track training: while this early education does give these particular horses a head start in their riding horse educations (should they retire from the track early), it also imposes more pressure and physical strain at a young age. Plus, so much time indoors early in life encourages some horses to develop bad habits, and a few act out because they are asked to do too much, too soon. Conscientious trainers notice this and withdraw such anxious horses from the sales prep or regular training, opting instead to turn them out to pasture for a while and re-enter the training program later in their two-year-old year. However, some trainers push their horses ahead and deal with the consequences later.

Breaking and Training

A lot of money is at stake in the racing industry, and horses don't earn their keep by standing around in the barn. While trainers of other breeds and in other disciplines allow young horses to fully mature before being ridden—many Warmbloods are not started under saddle until age three or four—many Thoroughbreds are started in training as early as October of their yearling year. (Note: all Thoroughbreds, no matter what month of the year they are born, are given a birth date of January 1, and so it goes without saying that foals born later in any given year are at a disadvantage.) Of course, not all racehorse trainers impose the same time frame and, as I mentioned in the section on prepping two-year-olds for sales, some do employ a slightly

slower training process in order to minimize stress on their horses.

Breaking on the Farm

Thoroughbreds are started under saddle using a variety of methods, just as there are many approaches to backing pleasure or show horses. Each trainer or owner has his own philosophy on how the breaking process should go. Some training farms do a month of groundwork, teaching the horse to be longed and ground driven before he is backed. A few farms do "sacking out" or desensitizing exercises in the round pen.

As with other breeds and disciplines, during early training the young Thoroughbred is first taught to wear a saddle and bridle, then carry a rider. Usually a couple of handlers are present the first time the horse is mounted. In the ideal scenario, they work very slowly with the horse, lifting the rider onto the horse's back in a calm and matter-of-fact series of events.

With the rider on and a handler on the ground at all times, the horse's training under saddle starts in a round pen or small arena. After learning to walk and trot he is taken to a training track, probably accompanied by a "pony horse" the first several times out. After that, young horses go out in groups and just jog around the track. Once they are comfortable jogging, the exercise riders let them canter.

For most horses, all of this is accomplished in about 100 days. At that point if a horse shows enough physical maturity and potential the trainer continues his program and starts working him at faster speeds. Physically and mentally immature horses are sometimes turned back out to pasture for a couple of months and resume their training in early fall.

Trainers at "quality" farms take this kind of extra time and work with each young horse at his own comfort level, but unfortunately, there are some trainers who mold a horse to their timetable rather than fit the program to each horse. These horses end up training on the track, whether they're ready or not.

1.5 Some farms take the time to incorporate ground-driving in their young Thoroughbred training program, allowing horses to be prepared for work under saddle without incurring undue stress and strain.

The Importance of Preparing for the Track

Life at the track is fast-paced and busy. Without sufficient preparation for the transition from the farm to this new environment, the experience can be so stressful that some horses never really recover. At New Vocations, we have seen a few of these cases—horses that were so mentally damaged they could not be transitioned.

It seems like common sense that a sufficiently trained and well-broken horse will have a better chance of racing successfully. Unfortunately, many owners do not know enough about racehorse training to realize that spending more money up front gives a horse a better chance of winning. While I have met many wonderful owners who make sure that their horses receive a solid

1.6 "Pony" horses are regularly used in training to help young Thoroughbreds gain confidence on the track.

1.7 A–J   When working with an OTTB, it is important to consider the life he lived as a racehorse-in-training. The backstretch is a busy yet highly structured environment, which is why most OTTBs appreciate and thrive on a steady routine (A). On and around the track, there are rules for everything. Horses are walked to and

foundation before going to the track, I have also met some who do not want to, or cannot afford to invest the time or money to get a Thoroughbred started well. For example, I have seen two-year-olds with only 30 days of training under saddle end up at the track. Often these horses end up being extremely nervous and develop bad habits that will persist after they retire from racing.

It is often hard to determine the actual experiences of an ex-racehorse, but when we receive an extremely nervous horse at New Vocations, chances are he was improperly and impatiently trained as a youngster. In such situations, our policy is to take him back to square one and begin again with work on the ground and in the round pen to give him a solid foundation before asking anything

from their workouts, some with a handler, while others can be ridden on a loose rein (B). Once on the track, jogging is limited to track space *off* the inside rail (C), as are slow steady gallops by single horses and their rider (D).

more demanding. (I discuss this process in detail beginning on p. 93.)

A Day at the Racetrack

It benefits everyone interested in owning an ex-racehorse to know what happens during a typical day at the track. If you have the opportunity to spend a morning hanging out behind the scenes, arrive really early and observe as much as possible. Remember that racehorses are not pets but high-performance athletes in training for one thing only: to win races. Respect their space and the instructions of those who work around and with them.

Trainers control and monitor every aspect of their charges' day. As you walk

E

F

Daily gallops are sometimes performed in pairs or small groups (E), while faster "workouts" usually involve two horses on the inside rail (F). After exercise, horses are bathed and hand-walked (G), and their legs wrapped for protection and support (H & I).

G

H

The One-Sidedness Myth

It is a common misconception that Thoroughbreds only know how to travel to the left; racehorses are actually trained and exercised in both directions around the track—although it is true they only race and perform their high-speed workouts going to the left.

During a race, horses change their "leading" leg several times: on the straightaways they gallop on the right lead, and then they change to the left lead for turns, which helps them get around, in balance, faster. This way, each leading leg and shoulder is intermittently rested so that the horse has more power to gallop. This also prevents them from only developing strength and tone on one side of the body.

When I was younger I worked at a training farm exercising horses, and we would alternate direction each day in order to develop equal muscle strength and balance in the horses. For example, on Monday all riders would gallop and jog to the left and then on Tuesday we would do the same to the right. We were able to organize in this manner because it was a private facility rather than a public track, and we did not have to worry about other trainers' workout schedules. Many farms with private tracks do the same.

for exercise. Young horses are accompanied by a rider on a "pony horse," or they will follow another, more experienced racehorse to the track.

Individual training programs depend on the trainer, but typically, youngsters are worked in pairs, which gives both horses confidence. Horses gearing up to be raced go out daily for a short gallop of about 1 to 2 miles total, starting and finishing with a jog to warm up and cool down. The gallop is not too fast: the goal is for the horse to stay in control and maintain a consistent pace. Most horses just "exercising"—jogging or galloping—will do so on the outside rail to both the right and the left (those going to the right will hug the outside rail, and those going left will stay just off the outside rail more toward the middle of the track). The inside rail is reserved for workouts: short, fast, timed gallops, to the left, generally with another horse to fuel competitive instincts. As you can see, morning workouts are organized chaos!

After exercise, horses are bathed and hand-walked to cool down. Once cool, the horses' legs are wrapped for protection and support. Under the bandages, a poultice or liniment is generally used for a cooling effect, or a "sweat" may be applied to reduce inflammation. There are many topical applications that are commonly used to "sweat" the leg, both home remedies and over-the-counter products. One combination typically found

around the backstretch where the stables are, you'll see that the horses are on a strict routine. Feeding and mucking-out starts around 4:30 or 5:00 A.M. Horses are exercised by 11:00 A.M. each day: in summer it is too hot to work them later, and during racing season the track is to be closed in preparation for afternoon or evening races. Some horses are hand-walked or put on a hotwalker to stretch their legs, while others are tacked-up and walked out to the track on the track is DMSO and nitrofurazone, which is rubbed on the lower legs and then covered in both plastic wrap and a regular standing wrap for support and pressure.

Back in the stables, horses are fed lunch at noon and are hand-walked again around 2:00 or 3:00 P.M. (Racehorses are rarely turned out unless at a training farm with round pens or small paddocks.) They are fed dinner between 5:00 and 6:00 P.M.—unless horses are racing, there is not a lot of other activity in the evening. At 4:30 A.M. the next day, the routine starts all over again.

Because of these long-established rhythms of the track, racehorses feel most comfortable, and therefore more confident, when their schedule follows a consistent routine. When the routine is altered too quickly, many become nervous or agitated. One trainer told me, "My horses are used to being led outside the barn where they wait while the exercise riders are thrown on their back. The horses then turn right and follow a path to the track. One day, there was some construction and the horses had to turn left and take a different path. Many of them acted as if they were not even 'broke'! They simply did not know what to do when their routine was changed."

This story demonstrates how you can never underestimate the importance of routine when working with an ex-racehorse, *especially* one right off the racetrack!

Race Day

Horses may race as often as once a week, once a month, or several times a year. How often the horse races is determined by his owner and trainer, who also decide the type and length of races, and whether he will run on dirt or turf.

Horses not permanently stabled at the track are usually shipped in on race day. During a race, the stable area is a "high-security"

A Racehorse's Typical Schedule*

4:30–5:00 A.M.   Feeding and mucking out
6:00–11:00 A.M.   Walking or exercising on the track, followed by bathing, hand-walking until cool, and grooming
12:00 P.M.   Midday feed
2:00–3:00 P.M.   Hand-walking
5:00–6:00 P.M.   Evening feed

*Every detail concerning each horse is monitored and changes to his schedule are made as necessary.

area—only those directly involved with the horses, or those with special permission, are allowed to be there. This prevents random onlookers from getting in the way of preparations, and is also a safety measure against foul play—a worry wherever betting is involved.

If you have every seen a race in person, or even on television, you have witnessed the incredible amount of activity a Thor-

RACE DAY

1.8 A–E Thoroughbreds are paraded and saddled in the Paddock on Race Day. There it is a hubbub of activity as grooms, jockeys, owners, and trainers make last minute preparations—all within reach of the spectators (A–C).

oughbred is exposed to before, during, and after a race. About 30 minutes before a race, handlers, followed by the grooms and owners, lead the horses to the "Paddock." The Paddock tends to be a grassy space with a circular path around the perimeter, usually enclosed by a short fence or hedge. Here the horses are saddled, walked, and mounted by their jockey. Although only trainers, owners, and those with special permission are allowed in the Paddock prior to a race, it is typically crowded with people and often chaotic. Large numbers of spectators surround the area, and people hang over the fence trying to get a look at the horses before they place their bets.

Most Paddocks have open-faced "saddling stalls" where the horses are tacked-up after they are paraded around the perimeter and the trainer gives the go-ahead. It is common to see horses appear anxious and buck or dance around as their girths are tightened. The trainers then do a last-minute check of the horse's condition and equipment themselves.

Once saddled, the horses are again paraded around the Paddock in their race order until they meet up with their jockey, who is

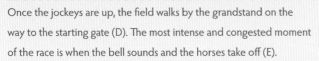

Once the jockeys are up, the field walks by the grandstand on the way to the starting gate (D). The most intense and congested moment of the race is when the bell sounds and the horses take off (E).

lifted on board. The field is then escorted to the track by a "lead horse." When they reach the track, the ground handlers release their charges to handlers on horseback—and then follows the familiar scene of the field parading in front of the grandstand.

Some horses jog toward the starting area, while others do a slow gallop and then a quick warm-up. As Post Time—when all race entries are due at the starting post—draws near, all the horses are called to their gate, where ground handlers are on hand to assist the jockeys. As soon as the last horse is securely loaded, the bell rings, and they're off!

Right out of the gate there is a lot of action and commotion as jockeys fight for a good position. Most of the horses will be part of a tight pack, with all but those in front getting dirt or mud thrown in their faces. Through it all, jockeys are talking or yelling, whips are swinging, and the crowd is screaming at the finish line.

Depending on the length of the race, most will be over in about two minutes (one of the amazing aspects of the sport is how much time and training goes into preparing for such a brief exercise in power). While the first horse over the finish line (barring disqualification or a challenge) is ridden directly to the Winner's Circle, the rest of the field heads to an exit gate where their grooms and trainers meet them. There, the jockeys hop off and the horses are quickly stripped of their saddles, and then sponged or hosed down before they are walked back to the barn. At the barn they are fully untacked and thoroughly bathed, then walked until cool.

Once the final order of the field is declared official, the first- and second-place horses have their blood and urine tested for illegal drugs.

Before being fed and put away for the night, horses that raced are examined and their legs are wrapped to keep any inflammation at bay. With a thick layer of bedding and plenty of hay, they are then left alone to recover from a stressful day.

Researching the Horse's History

When you first find an OTTB that you feel could be right for you, it is unlikely that you will know very much about his past. Nevertheless, with a little research, you may be able to get some valuable background information on his previous experiences.

The Jockey Club has a very helpful Web site, www.equineline.com, where you can look up any registered Thoroughbred's race record, sale information, and pedigree. All you need is the horse's registered name or registered number, which is tattooed under his upper lip (absence of a tattoo means the horse was never raced). I've listed below some of the facts that may be deduced from the information provided by the Jockey Club.

▶ Pedigree and Stud Fee

As with any breed, examining a Thoroughbred's pedigree can tell you a lot about the horse's potential character and athleticism. You may be able to find additional information about his dam and sire, as well as their other offspring, that can help you determine a horse's trainability, competitiveness, and physical longevity.

In addition, take the time to look up the sire's stud fees for an idea of how much was initially invested in the horse (check www.bloodhorse.com/stallion-register). If a large stud fee was paid—say, $10,000 or more—it is more likely the mare's owner had the funds to train and care for her foal properly, thus limiting the chances of stress-related mental trauma and physical injury. (Granted, this is a generalization, but it often holds true.)

▶ Purchased at Sales

A horse that was prepped for the Weanling or Yearling Sales tends to have better ground manners, since this ensures he was handled thoroughly at a young age. While he could certainly have acquired bad habits living at the racetrack, at least you know he had an early education.

Are Racehorses Abused at the Track?

People often ask me whether racehorses are mistreated. It is a subject that I've had many years to ponder—my father is a fifth-generation Standardbred trainer, and I grew up watching him work with his horses. He always handled them with respect, and though he wasn't overly sentimental in his dealings with them, he did everything within his means to keep his string happy and in good health. And, I believe that he is an example of the norm, rather than an exception.

During my tenure at New Vocations, I have worked with and met many different racehorse trainers from all over the country. As can be found in any division of the horse world, there are those with the animal's interests at heart, and those with more questionable ethical standards. I can honestly say that I have encountered more trainers who truly care about the well-being of their racehorses than those who do not.

However, there is a dichotomy in care and/or management within the racing industry, and this is most easily noted when you compare one track to another. At the larger, more prominent tracks, purses are much bigger and the competition greater, which in turn draws owners and trainers who have more money to work with. At this type of track, a "daily training fee" (which the trainer charges the owner and includes feed, board, grooming, and training, but neither veterinary nor farrier care) ranges from $75 to $125 a day. More money allows the barns to be better staffed, with more grooms and riders, high quality feed and hay, and the very best in vet and farrier care.

At smaller tracks, purses aren't worth as much, which attracts owners with fewer resources and less valuable horses. Here, the daily training fee can range from $15 to $50, which means many stables are understaffed and overworked. Exercise riders may groom, too. Trainers may have to clean stalls. Horses are more likely to be exercised on a mechanical hotwalker because there is less time (and fewer bodies) for hand-walking.

The difference here can become problematic for the horses; for example, in the case of minor injury. When there is money available, there is no hesitation to x-ray or examine further the location of any unusual swelling or heat. At a smaller track, limited funds often mean such problems are never diagnosed properly—until it is too late and the horse breaks down.

That said, even at the lowest of lower-tier tracks, I have met trainers who would rather go hungry than let their horses miss a meal. At the end of the day, a racehorse is still an investment and owners and trainers will generally do whatever they can to protect a horse's health during his racing career.

The other thing to rate is the horse's sales price. As is the case with stud fees (see p. 24), when a horse was purchased for a significant amount of money—$20,000 and up—at these sales, it is usually a sign that the new owner had the means necessary to ensure quality care and training as the horse was prepared for his racing career.

▶ Race Record

In my experience, a horse that has won a stakes race or earned over $100,000 at the track is often very intelligent. It takes a "good mind" and that little "something special" to successfully compete at this level, as well as the ability to understand "when to make it count." If a horse could handle the high stress of racing and come out a winner, this often means he is likely to catch on to new training quickly. While of course this is not always the case, at New Vocations we have seen time and again that stakes winners or big money earners are easier to transition to riding horses.

The other component here is that successful racehorses have often enjoyed the very best in care and handling. Trainers and owners will often go out of their way to keep a horse of such value happy and healthy.

► Frequency of Race Outings

Find out how often and how many times the horse raced. This information alone can tell you a lot about your OTTB.

If a horse never raced, he is less likely to have soundness issues down the road—his joints, ligaments, and tendons haven't suffered the "pounding" a seasoned competitor's have (though keep in mind he may never have raced *because* of soundness issues). The flip side is these horses haven't been exposed to "life on the track" to the same degree as those with racing experience. They may not be as accustomed to day-to-day handling, and they may have a more difficult time adjusting to a new environment.

Horses that have seen the start 15 or fewer times (generally the equivalent of two years of racing, or less) are accustomed to being groomed, bathed, wrapped, and ridden daily. They have been "tested" and

proven they have the fortitude to survive the racetrack—which may translate well to a new career. Of course, these horses have imposed more stress on their bodies and so are more likely to have sustained injury. They also may have developed bad habits on the ground or under saddle.

Horses that have raced for three to ten years have been shipped to countless racetracks, handled by many different grooms, and ridden by several jockeys. They have seen and experienced far more in that period of time than most horses do in their entire lives. If they leave the track without major injury or chronic unsoundness, I have found that chances are they will remain sound for most disciplines.

For some seasoned racehorses, however, it is difficult to transition to a new career; they have known one thing and one thing only—"being a racehorse." Because they have spent many years in a stall and unable to socialize with neighboring horses, some may have a hard time adjusting to turnout and/or participation in a community of horses. Plus, the wear-and-tear on their bodies will take a toll, and arthritis can develop earlier and to a greater degree than with horses that had a less lengthy racing career.

When you are looking at how often a horse raced, you may notice a "gap" of time—say three to 12 months—when nothing is on record. This often indicates a lay-up due to injury or time taken to rehabilitate the horse after surgery. Make special note of such "gaps"—while it may be impossible to find out the real reason for the time off, it can still help you understand an OTTB's history and warn you to pay careful attention to the veterinary exam.

▶ Location of Races

As mentioned on p. 25, it is good to note *where* a horse was raced. Larger, more recognized tracks can indicate a quality of training and attention to well-being that is harder to find at the smaller, lesser-known tracks where trainers are overworked, barns are understaffed, and financial resources tend to be limited.

Planning Ahead

People purchase or adopt a Thoroughbred with different intentions for the horse's future. Not everyone can be a full-time "horse person": family and work vie for time right along with the new horse. So, be fair to yourself and your horse—evaluate your time and your priorities *before* you bring an OTTB home. You need to be able to dedicate enough time to him to ensure a successful transition.

It is important that you take into account what is familiar to your OTTB so that you can understand his point of view as you help him adjust to his new lifestyle. This does not mean, however, that you have to keep a stakes winner in a "fancy" barn or ride only at 6:00 A.M. as the fog lifts—your OTTB will most likely adapt well to new circumstances. Patience and diligence go a long way toward helping your horse adjust to life after the racetrack.

Simple planning on your part eases the transition. Maintaining a regular feeding routine, turnout schedule, and exercise program are just the beginning—as you read the chapters that follow, I'll explain what you can expect from the OTTB and how to handle these, and other aspects of his segue from life at the racetrack to life as a riding horse.

2 End of the Race: Now What?

I have discussed how Thoroughbred breeders produce thousands of horses every year, and while most of these horses are indeed prepared and trained to run, only a select few go on to win prestigious races and vast sums of money—and only about 20 of them end up racing in the Kentucky Derby. Of those racehorses that make it to the starting gate, most have modest careers, perhaps bringing home enough winnings to cover their board and training. There are many different levels of racing: some races have a purse worth millions, some as little as $2,500. At smaller tracks you might see horses that are winning $50 each start for ten starts. Obviously, these horses need to find a new purpose in life, because they are definitely not paying the bills.

Reasons for Retirement

Most Thoroughbreds race for only a couple of years when they face an uncertain future. Successful or not, whether raced for two years or ten, each one is eventually "retired" from the track. A racehorse is retired for three main reasons: injuries sustained that affect his performance; loss of the "competitive edge"; or intended use for breeding.

Injury

Racehorses are most commonly injured as a result of several factors: a physical predisposition; training on poor track surfaces; improper shoeing; lack of fitness; or taking the notorious "bad step." While some of these can be prevented with correct care, others are simply the result of unavoidable circumstances and must be considered the risk taken when participating in a high-intensity sport.

Human athletes—professional and amateur—also experience injuries or soreness that they deal with regularly. Old injuries can persist throughout an athlete's lifetime, requiring long-term maintenance with oral medications, nutritional supplements, or alternative treatments like acupuncture and chiropractic. Thoroughbred trainers are used to treating their horses as athletes, and similar modes of care and therapy are employed. In addition, they work with veterinarians to rehabilitate horses and maintain soundness. Treatment options improve all the time, but veterinarians are not "miracle workers" and owners are not always willing, or able, to pay exorbitant costs for medical care.

To be fair, when it comes to injury there are many variables at play and many unknowns to consider: once experienced, an injury might heal, recur, and then become chronic, or it could never be a problem again. An injury might require surgery or other expensive treatment and rehabilitation, or it might be best to just leave it to heal on its own over time.

2.1 Most Thoroughbreds only race for a couple of years, then a lack of success on the track or injury means decisions must be made concerning their future.

Whatever the scenario, if an injury is treatable it always comes down to the same questions: will the horse be able to race again, and if so, how competitive will he be? In some cases, the expense of treatment in relation to these two all-important questions, rather than the severity of the injury, forces a horse's retirement.

Unfortunately, far too many horses that need surgery are retired from the track without adequate treatment. Many of these horses live the rest of their lives with chronic pain every step that they take. In some cases, the horse's quality of life is in question and it is debatable whether retirement is the right option or if the horse would be better off humanely euthanized. We take such cases very seriously at New Vocations and are not opposed to humanely euthanizing a horse that will be in pain the remainder of his life.

Competitive Decline

The sport of racing is not complicated to score: the first horse to finish wins! But even the successful horse can lose his edge, whether he starts to physically slow down or he loses the desire to win. In addition, some owners will only race at a high level, and refuse to consider less prestigious starts even if a horse is not performing well against tough competition. Horses that never win can actually be demoralized by consistently finishing near the back of the pack, and therefore lose their desire to even try. In any of these cases,

it is time for the owners to consider a new career for such horses, whether it is breeding for the more valuable animals (see below), or retirement as riding horses for the others.

Reproduction

A racehorse's retirement is not always due to lameness or loss of performance: Thoroughbred bloodlines can be a precious commodity, so some racehorses leave racing to stand at stud or become a broodmare. The more successful the horse's career and the better the pedigree, the more lucrative he or she is in the breeding shed.

At the higher end of racing, many horses are retired in good physical condition. When a horse is to become a breeding stallion, not only is the competitive race record important, he must also be healthy and sound. The same applies to a mare: she must have a healthy reproductive tract and be at least sound enough to carry a foal to term. A broodmare may produce one to even ten foals during her lifetime.

Retirement Options

Most trainers and owners cannot afford or do not want to spend time and money on a horse that is not a productive member of the racing string, so they begin considering their options as soon as it is decided to retire a horse from racing. These include sending

2.2 One viable option for OTTBs is becoming breeding stock. For example, this lovely Thoroughbred mare was approved to have Hanoverian foals.

the horse to a Thoroughbred breeding stock sale—a common choice for mares with good pedigrees and respectable race records—or selling him at a general all-breed auction. The latter are typically held at venues where other livestock are sold, as well, and happen on a weekly or bi-weekly basis. These are heavily attended by dealers who "flip" horses, buying them cheap and reselling them privately for more money, as well as buyers for slaughterhouses (see more about this issue on p. 33).

If an owner chooses not to sell a retired horse at auction, he may instead try to sell the horse himself (see p. 33), or send him to an adoption or rescue program, like New Vocations (see list on p. 245).

Becoming Breeding Stock

As mentioned, a mare with a decent race record or pedigree generally has value as a broodmare. A racehorse owner who is not involved in the breeding business will either sell the mare privately or through a breeding stock sale. However, a mare that does not have broodmare potential in the Thoroughbred industry may still be valuable for cross-breeding purposes—some wonderful sport

2.3 With so many Thoroughbred foals born each year, and so few going on to successful racing careers, it is difficult to find caring homes for those retired from the track. Thus, a crowded holding pen and eventual shipment to a slaughterhouse remains a possible fate for many.

horses have been the result of crosses with Quarter Horses, Paint Horses, Hanoverians, Oldenburgs, and American Warmbloods. Smaller Thoroughbred mares have become popular crosses with Welsh and other sport pony breeds.

Unfortunately, only a small number of Thoroughbred stallions are retired to stud. The Thoroughbred breeding industry is very competitive and it is difficult, if not impossible, for a racehorse that does not have an impressive pedigree or race record to join these ranks. And, unlike mares, few Thoroughbred stallions are crossed with other breeds.

Early in training, a colt with a good pedigree may be left a stallion in case he proves successful on the track, although no matter how fabulous the bloodlines, if he becomes unmanageable, he'll be gelded. Many colts with lesser pedigrees are gelded early on for just this reason—it makes them far easier to break and train to run. In direct relation to the value of the horses' pedigrees, you will tend to find more geldings racing at smaller tracks and more colts racing at bigger tracks.

Stallions have been sent to New Vocations in the past, ranging anywhere from three to nine years old, and in my experience they are easily transitioned to riding horses once they are gelded, probably because they were on the track and never actually used for breeding purposes.

Slaughter—The Grim Reality

According to the United States Department of Agriculture (USDA), in 2006, 100,800 horses (including healthy, sound racehorses) were slaughtered in the US. At the time of publication there have been many recent efforts to ban this practice completely in the US, with some success; however, there is still a demand for horse meat in the world market. This means horses are now being shipped to Canada and Mexico for slaughter purposes—both borders have seen an increase in numbers since US plants closed down.

Slaughter is a grim reality in the racing industry. With so many Thoroughbred foals born each year and only a limited number of people willing and able to take them when their racing career ends, it is difficult to find them a safe and caring new home. While plenty of buyers are people with good intentions, there are many horse dealers who frequently visit racetracks to buy horses at low prices—sometimes only a few hundred dollars—and then send them to an auction to make a quick buck. Owners, too, sometimes send retired horses to be sold at auction, which I discussed on p. 31. There, horses are sometimes purchased by private owners, but more often by horse dealers who ship them directly to the slaughterhouse.

Trainers often sell a horse unaware of its future. Perhaps they need to move the horse to make room for another horse in training, or they just need the money, and dealers normally offer cash and can take the horse away on the day of purchase. Sadly, though, horse slaughter is not always the result of "crooked dealing"; too often a trainer gives a horse to a family or person that lacks the skills needed to transition the horse to "normal" life. The new owner gets frustrated with the horse and the difficulties many present as a result of their race training, and start to look for someone—anyone—to take the horse off their hands. Some horse dealers seek out such opportunities, and invariably good horses end up going to slaughter for no reason.

For Sale by Trainer: Finding a Horse at the Track

On any given day, at most racetracks, there are a number of retired horses for sale. Prices can run the gamut—I've seen them range from as low as $300 to $5,000. Trainers with horses for sale usually put the word out by contacting dealers or buyers they've worked with before; some even list their horses on the Internet (www.equine.com, www.dreamhorse.com, and www.canterusa.org, for example) or in a local newspaper.

Plenty of people find success purchasing a horse directly from a trainer, but the majority of these are accomplished horsemen who may make their living retraining Thoroughbreds for resale and know how to identify a good riding prospect even when he is racing fit (and without getting on his back). Some have developed good relationships

2.4 A & B Thoroughbreds are often sold by trainers directly from the track. If arranged ahead of time, they will usually agree to show prospects to an interested buyer, set horses up outside their stall so you can examine their conformation, and allow a physical exam to be performed.

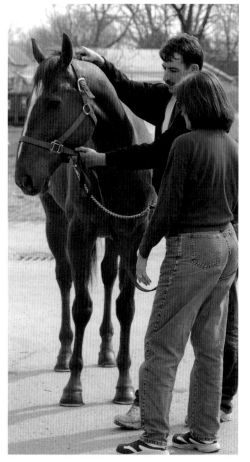

with Thoroughbred trainers and are able to work regularly with them to find what they are looking for.

If you are an experienced horse person, and you would like to buy a Thoroughbred directly from a trainer at the racetrack, please consider the following suggestions:

▸ Go before 11:00 A.M. when trainers are still at the barn. Most racetracks have a security gate—some are very open to visitors, while others may require a trainer meet you and escort you to the barns, so you may want to call ahead to find out.

▸ Be sure not to interrupt the morning schedule, but do let trainers know why you are there. Most will be happy to show you the horses they have for sale when they have a free moment.

► Ask a lot of questions. Make a list in advance, which should include the types of things you would like to know about *any* potential riding horse (see sidebar).

► Do a thorough leg evaluation (see p. 45). Often a trainer will not disclose the horse's entire health history, but will allow you to look over the horse's legs to check for any major blemishes or sign of injury. (Note: Most horses will have their legs wrapped, but this does not necessarily mean that the horse is injured. Many wear stable bandages daily for protection and support. Others, however, are wrapped to protect an injury or keep swelling down.)

► Beware the use of nonsteroidal anti-inflammatory drugs (NSAIDs) like phenyl-butazone ("bute"), which are often administered to horses. Bute helps reduce minor swelling, aches, and pain, so can "mask" an injury. Some trainers will tell you whether a horse is on bute while others will not.

► Most likely you will not be allowed to ride a horse—nor would you want to! However, trainers are often willing to set up a time for a second visit to see the horse jog or gallop with an exercise rider on board.

► If you plan to buy a horse, bring cash with you. Trainers will be more likely to lower prices for a cash sale rather than a check.

Questions to Ask when Viewing Horses at the Track

Take notes! And keep in mind that there may be a varying degree of truth to the answers you receive.

What is the horse's registered name and how do you spell it?
How long have you had the horse in your stable?
Can you tell me a little about his racing history? How many races? Where were they run? When was his last race?
Has the horse been injured? If so, when? Has the horse been raced since?
When was the horse's last workout?
How is he to exercise on the track?
Does the horse require a special bit or equipment, such as blinders?
What are his stall manners like?
Has the horse been on steroids?
Have any of his joints been injected? Which ones, and when?
Does he have any problematic behaviors or vices?
When was the horse gelded? (If applicable.)

The Adoption Option

New Vocations and other adoption programs were founded because many owners and trainers needed a safe place to send their ex-racehorses. I highly respect those who take the time to find an adoption program or retirement home for horses they no longer wish to keep. This is a far better decision than some of the examples I mentioned earlier—giving the horse to a ten-year-old girl who wants her first horse, or selling cheap to a horse dealer who then resells the horse to an unsuitable home or a slaughterhouse.

Which Thoroughbred Best Fits My Needs?

If you intend to purchase a horse off the track, or adopt through a program, I recommend you engage the assistance of an experienced friend or trainer to help ascertain the horse's suitability for you and your discipline. Even if you buy and sell horses all the time, a second opinion is always of value.

The most important step is to ask yourself what level of riding or competition you aspire to, as many OTTBs are athletic enough to pursue any discipline at the lower levels, and most minor injuries will hold up after proper time off. With this in mind, here are a few additional guidelines to consider when evaluating OTTBs. These are generalized suggestions—there is a lot more to consider when choosing a horse for a specific discipline. And note, the examples pictured here are "right off the track." Appearance changes with added weight and muscle.

The Event Horse or Jumper* (fig. 2.5 A)
Conformation
- High shoulder point (the front of the shoulder is high, with a steeply angled humerus from there to the elbow; this ensures scope over large jumps)
- Uphill build
- Medium bone structure (extremely fine bone structure is less likely to hold up)
- Short- to medium-length back
- Short- to medium-length pasterns (long pasterns tend to break down)
- Well-set knees (horses "straight" in the knees are prone to knee injuries)
- Event horses can range in height. Note that larger horses (in height and mass) can be more difficult to keep sound as they are harder on their legs and feet.

Movement
Event horses need to be very athletic with fluid gaits. Prospects should have more "action" at all three gaits than, say, a hunter (see right). This often indicates it will be easier for them to move with impulsion in the dressage ring and that they will pick up their knees better over fences.

Personality
- Brave · Athletic · Hard-Working

Event prospects need to be bold, brave, and forward-going horses that have good endurance. Many of these horses could also be described as "proud" or "arrogant." More energetic horses are often possibilities—as long as they are mentally sane and have a good work ethic, the extra energy is beneficial on the cross-country course.

Injuries to Avoid
- Breathing issues
- Severe tendon injuries (mild strains or bows are generally not an issue if given enough time off prior to retraining)
- Severe suspensory injuries
- Joint chips or fractures
- Vision limitations

*A jumper prospect will be very similar in build, action, and personality to an event horse. When looking for a jumper, put more emphasis on a stronger hind end and shoulder. A jumper does not necessarily need to be built uphill, but he should have a high shoulder point.

The Hunter (fig. 2.5 B)
Conformation
- Long, sloping shoulder
- Neck ties in well with the withers and shoulder
- Small, attractive head
- Flat topline

Movement
Hunters should be light on their feet and have as little action in their legs as possible. A long, low, rhythmic stride that easily covers a lot of ground is desirable. The horse's head carriage should be long and low.

Personality
- Easygoing · Consistent · Stylish

Hunters are judged on rhythm, style, and manners. They need to be calm in nature and consistent in gait and attitude as they move around the ring and over fences.

Injuries to Avoid

- Severe tendon injuries (mild strains or bows are generally not an issue if given enough time off prior to retraining)
- Severe suspensory injuries
- Joint chips or fractures

The Dressage Horse (fig. 2.5 C)

Conformation

- Withers set back from the shoulder
- Short back
- Uphill build
- Strong, well-built hindquarters
- Neck ties in well with the withers and shoulder (avoid ewe-necked horses)
- Neck should be medium to long

Movement

The horse should naturally engage and drive from his hind end. A regular, even, four-beat walk is ideal. At the trot he should demonstrate natural impulsion and extension while remaining light on his feet. Look for a canter that is not overly "large"—a shorter stride is easier to maneuver around the dressage arena and eventually teach clean flying lead changes.

Personality

- Hard-Working · Sensitive · Sensible

A dressage prospect should be a sensitive yet sensible horse. He needs to be very responsive to leg, seat, and rein aids rather than dead-sided or hard-mouthed. He cannot become overwrought every time he is confronted with a new task—the ideal horse likes to work and accepts new challenges eagerly.

Injuries to Avoid

- Severe tendon injuries (mild strains or bows are generally not an issue if given enough time off prior to retraining)
- Severe suspensory injuries
- Joint chips or fractures

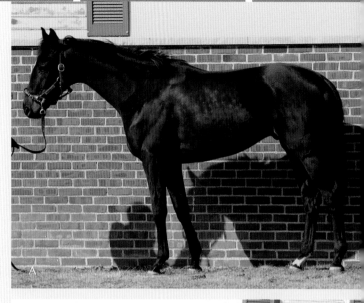

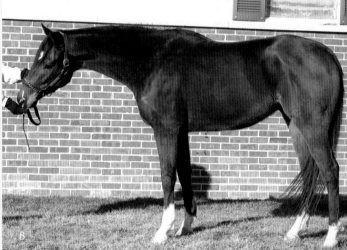

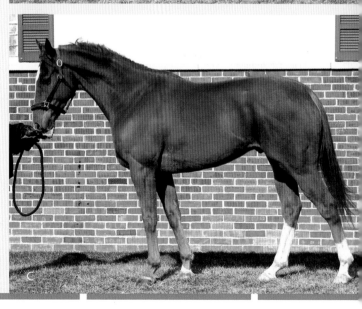

Ferdinand's Story

Winner of the 1986 Kentucky Derby and the 1987 Breeders' Cup Classic, Ferdinand was voted the 1987 Horse of the Year. He won eight of 29 starts and earned $3,777,978, retiring at the time as the fifth leading-money-earner on record. Following his racing career, Ferdinand stood at stud for several years in the US. Then in 1994, he was sold and sent to Japan to stand at stud. To the disbelief and dismay of many, Ferdinand was sold to slaughter by the Japanese breeding farm in 2002 when he was no longer needed as a breeding stallion.

By adopting or purchasing a Thoroughbred off the racetrack you can give a horse a chance to excel in a new career rather than end up at a slaughterhouse. To learn more about this issue, see my discussion on p. 33, or view the Equine Protection Network Web site at www.equineprotectionnetwork.com or the American Horse Protection Coalition Web site at www.horse-protection.org.

The problem faced by many of the adoption and retirement programs in the US today is that there are more horses in need of new homes than there are programs with room. One of my goals in writing this book is to encourage the person who is looking for a Thoroughbred to work with an adoption program. As I mentioned, it is extremely difficult for the average horseman to evaluate a horse at the track and know if it will be suitable for his needs. Once a racehorse has been moved to an adoption program's facility, he has already taken the first steps necessary to transition him from the track to a new career, and you will be able to get a much better feel for his potential as a riding horse.

There are many advantages to working with an adoption or retirement program. For example, once at New Vocations, an ex-racehorse is:

▸ Evaluated for mental health and physical condition, and veterinary advice is given on request.

▸ Worked on the ground and under saddle and judged for suitability as a riding horse in different disciplines.

▸ Fed a suitable diet. Thin or race-fit horses receive extra calories to promote weight gain.

▸ Introduced to turnout in paddocks or fields and offered opportunities to relearn how to socialize with others—something he probably hasn't done since he was a foal.

▸ Provided "transitional" training and a potential adopter can then see him being worked from the ground and under saddle.

Adoption Costs

Every program handles this element differently. At New Vocations, we aim to keep our fees low as we all know how prohibitive the costs of boarding and caring for a horse can be! We feel that the money is better spent if the adopter can put it toward the OTTB's training and care. By placing New Vocations horses quickly, we limit the amount of money we put into them (feed, farrier, vet), which in turn allows us to keep our fees affordable.

Our fees range from $0 to $700. We will ask $700 for a fairly young, sound horse, and lower the fee accordingly if an animal is limited by injury or if he has a vice such as cribbing or weaving. We waive fees completely for most horses 15 and older, those that have an injury that requires rehabilitation or stall rest prior to the beginning of training, and horses that have behavioral issues that require extra time and attention.

Tips for Adopting an OTTB

As I stated earlier, getting your horse from an adoption program has many benefits. But, it helps to be clear about what you want before you begin the process. Here are some general tips to help you through the process:

▸ Read through the specific policies and procedures of the adoption program. Each program works slightly differently when placing their horses and many have an application process.

▸ Read the adoption contract or agreement thoroughly and ask plenty of questions so that you can be completely clear about what commitments you will have to make (see sidebar). Adoption programs vary. Some, like New Vocations, will always accept a horse back, should the placement not work out; others only do so for a certain length of

---

Questions to Ask when Adopting an OTTB

Note: see also the questions to ask when buying horses at the track, p. 35.

How long has the horse been off the track?
How long has he been in the program?
What can you tell me about his racing history and pedigree?
Did he come from the track or a farm? Which one?
Why did he retire from racing?
Does he have any old or current injuries? Has the vet evaluated him?
Has the horse been on any medication or supplements?
What is he being fed? How much?
What training has he received so far? Has he started under saddle?
How is he adjusting to turnout? How is he with other horses?
How is the horse to groom, tack-up, and otherwise work around?
Does he tie/cross-tie?
What kind of bit is he ridden in?
How does he travel?

---

time. Some forbid you from ever selling the horse; others permit you to sell it after a certain period of time; still others request "first right of refusal" should you decide to sell.

▸ Consider what your overall goals will be for the adopted horse. If you know you want to ride for pleasure or compete in a specific discipline, it is extremely helpful to share your preferences with the adoption program in order for the staff to match you with an appropriate horse.

- If you are planning to work with a specific trainer, involve him in the whole adoption process and have him accompany you to view any potential horses.

- Be honest and very clear with the staff regarding your previous experience with horses. You will only be cheating yourself if you claim to know more than you actually do, as they need an accurate picture of your abilities to ensure that you are matched with a suitable horse.

- If you feel that you do not have enough experience but would still like to adopt, plan to send the horse to a trainer for the first several months, then have the trainer assist you with the rest of the training process.

- Set up a time to visit the horse when you can see him ridden (most programs have someone familiar with the animal on hand when an adopter visits), and, if you are a good enough rider and the program allows it, try him yourself.

- If you are considering a horse with a known injury, consult your veterinarian (or find one near you) for suggestions on rehabilitation before taking him on. Most programs disclose information about a horse's injuries and give advice about rehabilitation.

Adoption Programs

Many programs are available that offer retired racehorses for adoption. I recommend thorough research to find one with policies that fit your needs before you make a commitment. You can find a list on p. 245 of some reputable organizations that focus either entirely or partially on placing OTTBs in new homes.

2.6 Adoption programs have many OTTBs looking for loving homes. Cracked Cup raced 100 times before being retired. He and his new owner, Julie Caldwell, now enjoy pleasure riding and competing in jumper shows.

3 Where Does It Hurt?

Common Lameness and Health Issues in OTTBs

Thoroughbreds are athletes and the extensive training that they undergo at a young age takes both a physical and mental toll. Racing itself puts tremendous physical strain on a horse's body as he pushes himself to peak performance again and again. Hoof and leg-related lameness are common, as is body soreness resulting from the stress and physical demands experienced on and around the track. It is no surprise then, that following retirement, most of these horses need some sort of treatment or physical therapy to speed recovery. In many cases, rest proves to be the best medicine, but there are a variety of care regimens that can help transition a horse's mind and body, and get him healthy.

Pre-Purchase Exams

The Adopted OTTB

As I recommended in the last chapter, before making a commitment, you can ask about a horse's health history, and in most cases you will get an honest and informed answer. However, most adoption programs do not have the finances to fully vet every horse that comes through the barn door—instead, veterinarians are called in to assess and treat major injuries or seek the causes of specific maladies. With this in mind, those adopting an animal with the intent to compete him at a high level may choose to have a "pre-purchase" exam done *before* they assume ownership—but do note it is the adopter's responsibility to have the horse checked if he feels it is necessary. At New Vocations, we encourage adopters to take the horse home and arrange to have their own vet look him over when the time and expense can be spared. In most cases, this is sufficient.

If you plan to pursue a discipline that demands more of your horse than casual pleasure riding—in other words, one that is physically demanding or involves obstacles—it is advisable to have a vet examine your horse *before* you begin his training program. This can include having his eyes, wind, and heart checked for irregularities, and if there is reason for concern, blood tests to determine if he is anemic or has any other deficiencies, and X-rays of all four feet.

The OTTB Purchased from the Track or at Auction

If you buy a horse directly from the shed row at the track there may not be an opportunity for a professional pre-purchase exam. Some trainers will allow an exam, and a track veterinarian may even be on hand to perform one, but more often than not, logistical issues will get in the way. Therefore, when you find a horse you like, it is a good idea to be prepared to assess his soundness yourself—unless you're looking for a pet or companion animal,

3.1 Recently retired Thoroughbreds can suffer from a number of health and lameness issues, so it is important to perform a general check for soundness before beginning a retraining program.

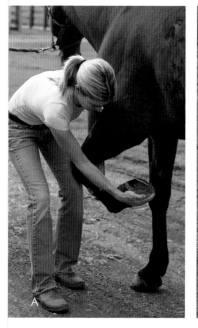

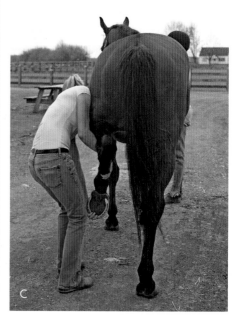

3.3 A–C Performing a flexion test on the fetlock (A), knee (B), and hock (C).

ing soft tissue structures are stretched and/ or compressed for a brief period of time by bending and holding the limb. The horse is then immediately trotted away. The process highlights any limitation in movement and soreness is more evident. A good comparison would be if you squatted down for a few minutes, then stood up and immediately started to run. You may be fine, or you may instead experience some soreness or initial stiffness, which could be attributed to a bad knee or an old ankle sprain, for example.

▶ Front Legs

To perform a flexion test on the front fetlock, ask the horse to pick up his hoof and prepare

him by gently moving his toe back and forth. Then flex the horse's toe toward the fetlock to compress the joint, and apply steady pressure for about 45 seconds (fig. 3.3 A). If the horse pulls away from you or flinches it may be an indication that he is experiencing discomfort in that area, although keep in mind that some horses may flinch the first time they are flexed just because of the unfamiliar pressure.

When the time is up, have your helper trot the horse forward immediately, in a straight line, as you watch for unevenness in his gait as he jogs away from you. Note any shortness or stiffness in his stride, head bobbing, or a reluctance to extend at the trot. Repeat the process for the other front fet-

Thoroughbreds are athletes and the extensive training that they undergo at a young age takes both a physical and mental toll. Racing itself puts tremendous physical strain on a horse's body as he pushes himself to peak performance again and again. Hoof and leg-related lameness are common, as is body soreness resulting from the stress and physical demands experienced on and around the track. It is no surprise then, that following retirement, most of these horses need some sort of treatment or physical therapy to speed recovery. In many cases, rest proves to be the best medicine, but there are a variety of care regimens that can help transition a horse's mind and body, and get him healthy.

Pre-Purchase Exams

The Adopted OTTB

As I recommended in the last chapter, before making a commitment, you can ask about a horse's health history, and in most cases you will get an honest and informed answer. However, most adoption programs do not have the finances to fully vet every horse that comes through the barn door—instead, veterinarians are called in to assess and treat major injuries or seek the causes of specific maladies. With this in mind, those adopting an animal with the intent to compete him at a high level may choose to have a "pre-purchase" exam done *before* they assume ownership—but do note it is the adopter's responsibility to have the horse checked if he feels it is necessary. At New Vocations, we encourage adopters to take the horse home and arrange to have their own vet look him over when the time and expense can be spared. In most cases, this is sufficient.

If you plan to pursue a discipline that demands more of your horse than casual pleasure riding—in other words, one that is physically demanding or involves obstacles—it is advisable to have a vet examine your horse *before* you begin his training program. This can include having his eyes, wind, and heart checked for irregularities, and if there is reason for concern, blood tests to determine if he is anemic or has any other deficiencies, and X-rays of all four feet.

The OTTB Purchased from the Track or at Auction

If you buy a horse directly from the shed row at the track there may not be an opportunity for a professional pre-purchase exam. Some trainers will allow an exam, and a track veterinarian may even be on hand to perform one, but more often than not, logistical issues will get in the way. Therefore, when you find a horse you like, it is a good idea to be prepared to assess his soundness yourself—unless you're looking for a pet or companion animal,

3.1 Recently retired Thoroughbreds can suffer from a number of health and lameness issues, so it is important to perform a general check for soundness before beginning a retraining program.

you probably won't want to bring a potentially crippled animal home just because you like his looks (see below for a soundness test). If you like the horse but you aren't confident in your own abilities to detect problems or unsoundness, bring a knowledgeable friend or your trainer to get a second educated opinion.

Some trainers are fairly honest about injuries (bowed tendons, quarter cracks, and bone chips, to give just a few examples), as they want to see a horse go to the most appropriate home. Other trainers just want to get the horse out of the way quickly, and even if he is clearly unsound, they may assure you, "He will be fine with some turnout." In these cases, the trainer may know where the horse is sore but may not know the full extent of the injury because he could not pay for X-rays—for example, the horse may have fetlock soreness so the trainer applied a sweat or "injected" it, when in reality there is a bone chip or fracture that would be best treated with surgery. Unfortunately, horse trading is *always* a "buyer beware" market.

And of course, if you pick up an OTTB at an auction, all bets are off!

Underlying Problems

As you transition your Thoroughbred, keep in mind that many behavioral issues you may automatically attribute to his upbringing at the track could instead be the result of discomfort. Before you reprimand him or lose patience, consider that he may have a physical problem your veterinarian can identify. Understanding that this is a possibility and having an idea of the kinds of pain and unsoundness poor behavior can indicate is an important attribute in an OTTB owner.

On the following pages, I address the following:

1 How to perform a soundness evaluation
2 Common race-related injuries
3 The use of anabolic steroids
4 How to deal with gastric ulcers
5 Common hoof issues
6 Recommended treatments for lameness
7 Alternative medicines and therapies

A Simple Soundness Evaluation

When a Thoroughbred arrives at New Vocations, we perform a general soundness exam before we incorporate turnout into his regimen or begin any training. A *sound* horse is free from injury, illness, or conformation defects that may impede his ability to perform at present or in the future. He moves without hesitation and does not limp or otherwise display pain or discomfort. Note that a horse may have an old injury that no longer affects him and still be deemed sound.

There is a lot that the average horseman can do to evaluate a horse's soundness, keeping in the back of your mind that you can consult a veterinarian if necessary. Below I've provided a description of how to perform a simple examination, either before you bring a new horse home or prior to starting work with him. I recommend you write down your observations so that if there appears to be a problem, you can thoroughly explain your findings to your vet.

General Impression

First of all, observe the horse and consider his general condition and attitude. Is he of normal weight for his height or ribby? Is his coat shiny or dull? Is his expression interested or lethargic? Anxious or worried? Does he stand square or with one foot pointing or trailing behind?

Legs

Next, check all four legs for obvious scars, cuts, swelling, or heat. Injuries commonly occur at the joints: knees and hocks, fetlocks and pasterns, as well as in the tendons located behind the cannon bones. Run your hands down each leg, starting at the top just below the elbow or stifle and working your way down to the hoof.

Compare the two front legs to each other and the two hind legs in the same manner to check for symmetry and to identify any irregularities. Compare the temperature of both front legs, noting if one is warmer than the other. Repeat behind. Heat is often an indication of inflammation or infection.

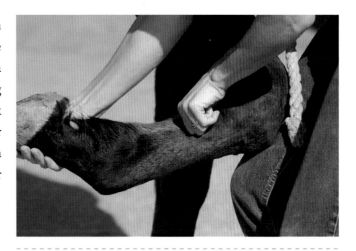

3.2 Palpating the tendons and ligaments behind the cannon bone can help reveal any soreness the horse is experiencing in that area.

Aside from obvious or subtle lameness, be alert to loss of limb flexibility (see below) or a painful response to palpation and/or manipulation of any area (fig. 3.2).

Flexion Tests

Flexion tests are commonly used to diagnose lameness in horses. Veterinarians usually perform flexion tests during regular pre-purchase exams, but any experienced horseperson with a good eye for lameness should be able to perform this test. A helper is required to trot the horse following flexion. (Caution: I do not recommend the novice horseman attempt these tests as they can be harmful to the horse and dangerous to the inexperienced handler.)

In flexion tests, joints such as the knee, fetlock, hock, and sometimes stifle (these are more difficult to flex), and correspond-

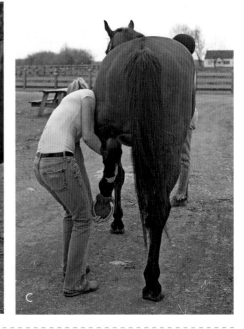

3.3 A–C Performing a flexion test on the fetlock (A), knee (B), and hock (C).

ing soft tissue structures are stretched and/ or compressed for a brief period of time by bending and holding the limb. The horse is then immediately trotted away. The process highlights any limitation in movement and soreness is more evident. A good comparison would be if you squatted down for a few minutes, then stood up and immediately started to run. You may be fine, or you may instead experience some soreness or initial stiffness, which could be attributed to a bad knee or an old ankle sprain, for example.

▶ Front Legs

To perform a flexion test on the front fetlock, ask the horse to pick up his hoof and prepare him by gently moving his toe back and forth. Then flex the horse's toe toward the fetlock to compress the joint, and apply steady pressure for about 45 seconds (fig. 3.3 A). If the horse pulls away from you or flinches it may be an indication that he is experiencing discomfort in that area, although keep in mind that some horses may flinch the first time they are flexed just because of the unfamiliar pressure.

When the time is up, have your helper trot the horse forward immediately, in a straight line, as you watch for unevenness in his gait as he jogs away from you. Note any shortness or stiffness in his stride, head bobbing, or a reluctance to extend at the trot. Repeat the process for the other front fetlock, and then for both knees. Flex the knees for 90 seconds before asking your helper to trot the horse off (fig. 3.3 B).

▶ Hind Legs

After you have flexed both front legs, proceed to the hind legs. They can be harder to evaluate, and unfortunately, some horses refuse to stand still for the appropriate flexion tests. Start by picking up one hind leg and pulling it gently forward, up toward the horse's belly (fig. 3.3 C). Hold it there for 90 seconds and then have your helper trot the horse off immediately. Watch for any irregularities of gait: dropping his hip more on one side than the other, "dragging his toes," shortness of stride, "trailing a hind leg," or bobbing his head. Horses that have soreness in their hocks, stifles, or hips will show discomfort during this test.

Flex the horse's hind fetlocks in the same way as the front fetlocks.

Feet

Take the time to also inspect each hoof. Look for cracks and chips in the outer wall and uneven areas of hoof growth. Pick the hoof up and look for signs of an abscess on the sole. Also check for signs of thrush, which appears as a dark and smelly substance especially around the frog. If the sole of the hoof appears unhealthy or abnormal, make note of your observations and consult your farrier.

Racehorses are shod with lightweight aluminum shoes called "racing plates" and often experience sensitivity and/or bruising when these shoes are first pulled. If you suspect a horse might be footsore, *hoof testers* can be used to apply pressure to the sole and heel (see p. 55 for more on how to use hoof testers).

Overall Body

Search for other possible sources of pain by running your hands over the horse's body. Run one hand along the horse's spine, then repeat, this time with only a couple of fingers and extra pressure. Do the same thing over the musculature on either side of his back and hindquarters (figs. 3.4 A & B). Watch the horse's body language. Notice if he flinches, throws his head up, pins his ears, or tries to bite, kick, or strike. These can all be indicators of discomfort or pain. Work carefully as you move around the horse and make sure you don't get in the way of his hooves or his teeth!

Many Thoroughbreds are sensitive from muscle soreness, while others are ticklish and will not like being touched all over. The way to tell the difference is to "desensitize" the area: if the horse is reacting to your initial touch, continue to stroke that area until he no longer objects. Then try applying slightly more pressure to the same area by using your thumb. If the horse reacts again, chances are he is sore.

3.4 A & B Check the horse's body for soreness, starting at the withers and moving slowly across the back using your thumb and index finger. Continue down the horse's rump.

When to Get Help

Minor issues may be resolved with rest and time, but if you suspect a serious injury, do not hesitate to call your veterinarian and get a professional opinion. While a simple soundness evaluation can give you a general idea of a horse's condition, veterinarians have an array of high-tech diagnostic tools, including—but not limited to—radiography, magnetic resonance imaging (MRI), computed tomography (CT), thermography, nuclear imaging (bone scans), ultrasound, and synovial fluid analysis, which can help determine the cause of just about any problem. In more complex cases, a vet's opinion is also necessary in determining the best plan for treatment and rehabilitation.

Injuries and Conditions Commonly Seen in OTTBs

While there are hundreds of ailments a horse can suffer from, I've included here a list of some of the most common injuries and conditions found in Thoroughbreds, usually incurred in race training or racing, along with possible treatments and prognoses. All of the injuries I have included can range dramatically in severity—those on the moderate end of the spectrum can often be successfully treated and rehabbed, and the affected horse can return to racing or go on to a new career.

3.5 Bucked shin

I recommend you keep a quality vet book that offers a more comprehensive list of maladies and therapies on hand for reference (see Resources, p. 245), and consult your veterinarian if your horse appears to be in pain or is slow in recovering from a previously diagnosed injury.

Bucked Shin

▶ Description: Inflammation, heat, and tenderness in the surrounding tissue of the cannon bone, similar to shin splints in humans (fig. 3.5). This is extremely prevalent in young racehorses in training.

▶ Cause: Usually concussion on immature legs.

▶ Treatment: Rest, cold-hosing, anti-inflammatory drugs, and ESWT (extracorporeal shockwave therapy) works wonders (it is used by many track vets and provides faster and more complete healing—see p. 61).

▶ Prognosis: Once the inflammation has subsided and/or the horse is no longer lame, he should be able to return to training. This varies according to the severity of the damage.

Tendonitis (Bowed Tendon)

▶ Description: Injury to a tendon causing inflammation of the tendon or tendon sheath, usually in the superficial digital flexor tendon or sometimes in the deep digital flexor tendon (fig. 3.6). Damage to the tendon can range from slight to severe depending on whether the tendon fibers have been stretched or torn, and to what degree.

▶ Cause: Strain due to low heels and long toes, poor conformation, deep footing, fatigue, hyperextension, or improper training.

▶ Treatment: Stall rest, support bandages, cold therapy, hydrotherapy, and anti-inflammatory drugs. In some cases, surgery is performed.

▶ Prognosis: Depends on severity of the injury and treatment chosen. Minor strains or tears in the tendon sheath may heal after only one to three months of rest. Major tears take longer—up to a year. The injured tendon

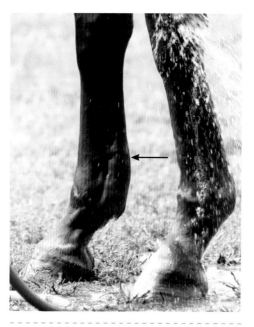

3.6 Tendonitis

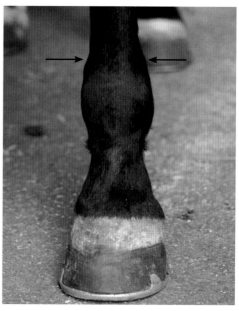

3.7 Strained suspensory ligament

should be ultrasounded by a vet and given the "all-clear" before the horse returns to work.

Strained Suspensory Ligament

▶ Description: Injury to the important suspensory ligament, which supports and stabilizes the fetlock and protects it from overflexing or twisting during exercise (fig. 3.7).

▶ Cause: Strain due to low heels and long toes, poor conformation, deep footing, fatigue, hyperextension, or improper training.

▶ Treatment: Stall rest, support bandages, cold-hosing, anti-inflammatory drugs, ESWT (see p. 61).

▶ Prognosis: Severe suspensory injuries usually require a year or more of rehabilitation, after which the horse will probably only be suitable for light pleasure riding. ESWT has been successful treating minor to moderate strains but not always severe injuries, which often include injury to tendons and sesamoids. Minor strains, tears, or lesions can be successfully rehabilitated in three to nine months depending on the degree of injury. Once healed, these horses are able to return to most types of riding and performance activity.

Splint

▶ Description: Injury to the splint bone, usu-

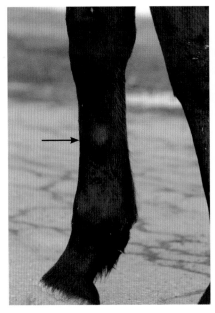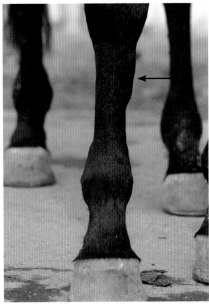

3.8 A & B Splints

ally on the inside of the cannon bone (called a *medial* splint) causing inflammation within the membrane covering the bone or supporting ligament (figs. 3.8 A & B). Eventual calcification in the area of the injury results in a bony enlargement on the side of the cannon bone.

▶ Cause: Strain due to concussion, poor conformation, fatigue, external trauma (i.e. a blow to the leg), or nutritional deficiency.

▶ Treatment: Rest, cold-hosing, and anti-inflammatory drugs. (ESWT has been known to be used on splints, as well.)

▶ Prognosis: Once healed, most splints be-

come "cosmetic" blemishes that do not affect the horse's soundness. Location of the splint can dictate whether or not it proves troublesome. It is common for a racehorse to sustain a splint, especially early in his training, but rarely do they prevent a horse from strenuous performance work later on.

Osselets

▶ Description: Inflammation of the joint capsule of the fetlock is known as "green" osselets (fig. 3.9). Chronic cases, often resulting in calcium buildup in both front fetlocks, are called "true" osselets.

▶ Cause: Concussion, poor conformation

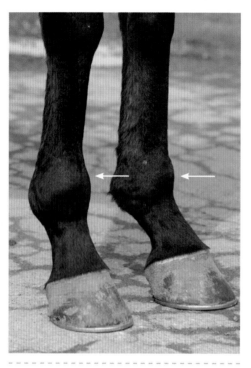

3.9 Osselets

(short, upright pasterns are more prone to osselets).

▶ Treatment: Rest, cold-hosing, anti-inflammatory drugs.

▶ Prognosis: Once calcified, most osselets are not painful. If calcification is minimal and does not occur within the joint, then the horse will be able to return to a normal workload. However, in severe cases, bony changes accumulate and arthritis limits the flexion of the fetlock, and the afflicted horse may only be suitable for limited performance or pleasure riding.

Sesamoid Fracture

▶ Description: Injury to the sesamoid bone at the back of the fetlock joint.

▶ Cause: Fatigue—injury often occurs at the end of a race or workout when the suspensory ligament gives way and the fetlock loses support in a misstep.

▶ Treatment: Depends on the location of the fracture. Some cases can return to moderate riding with several months of stall rest, accompanied by a cold-hosing regimen and wrapping. However, many require surgery: fractures or bone chips at the *top* of the sesamoid are easiest to repair; *middle* fractures normally need to be repaired with a screw; and fractures or chips at the *bottom* of the sesamoid are the worst case and have the poorest prognosis.

▶ Prognosis: Poor circulation to the sesamoid bone area impedes healing, and recovery is further complicated by the suspensory ligament, which is often involved in the injury. With or without surgery, most horses' futures are limited to flatwork.

Knee Fracture

▶ Description: Hairline or complete fracture in the knee, seen most commonly in the third carpal bone (fig. 3.10).

▶ Cause: Hyperextension of the leg caused

by poor conformation and/or fatigue, allowing the bones of the joint to collide.

▶ Treatment: A small or partial fracture may heal with six to eight weeks of stall rest; however, most of these injuries require surgery, followed by stall rest.

▶ Prognosis: Depending on the location and severity of the fracture, some horses have been rehabbed following surgery and returned to racing. More severe cases are likely to be able to resume work but at a reduced load. Eventually, arthritic changes in the joint may reduce flexibility and limit how much work the horse can tolerate.

Bone Chip (Knee or Fetlock)

▶ Description: A "chip fracture" or fragment that may or may not separate from the surface of the bone.

▶ Cause: Overtraining, trauma to the bone, poor conformation, defective bone development due to OCD (osteochondrosis).

▶ Treatment: Surgical removal and/or rest, depending on the location of the chip and how much trouble it is causing. Joint injections and anti-inflammatory drugs are commonly used in conjunction with those that are not removed; however, if the horse requires injections more than two or three times a year, surgery should be performed.

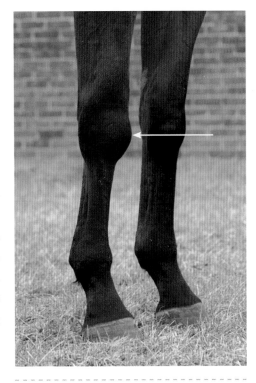

3.10 Knee fracture

▶ Prognosis: Many bone chips cause irritation and wear away at the cartilage in the joint. If a bone chip is causing lameness, it should be removed as early as possible to limit related arthritis or cartilage damage. In these cases, most horses are able to work at some level.

Common Hoof Issues in OTTBs

If a horse seems lame and neither heat nor swelling is apparent in the leg, the hoof is the next most obvious place to consider.

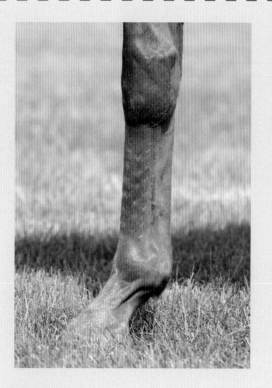

A Word on Pin Firing

It is not unusual for an OTTB to have small dot-like scars running up and down his cannon bones in several rows. These are the result of a procedure called **pin firing**. Though some people shy away from horses that have been pin fired, there are rarely long-term negative effects from this treatment. By the time the scar forms, the injury that was treated with pin firing should have healed and is not likely to reoccur. The horse can generally return to work.

Pin firing is commonly used on injuries such as splints, bucked shins, curbs (inflammation and/or tearing of the plantar tarsal ligament on the outside of the hock), or chronic bowed tendons. It is performed with a small, hot probe that burns the tissue of the injured or sore area. The purpose is to increase blood flow to the affected area, thereby promoting healing and regeneration of tissue.

Though pin firing has fallen out of favor with some people, others still use it as an inexpensive treatment.

Thoroughbreds tend to have sensitive feet with thin walls and soles, making them more prone to hoof problems than other breeds. Issues are exacerbated by the way farriers at the track tend to take off too much sole and trim the heels too low, supposedly because such trimming helps increase the length of the horse's stride. This theory is debatable, but what it *does* do is make horses even more susceptible to problems such as stone bruises, heel bruises, and hoof abscesses (see text to follow).

Bruises

If the sole of the hoof experiences unlevel or persistent impact, internal tissue can be damaged, resulting in a *bruise* that can often be identified by the accompanying discoloration. As mentioned, bruising can be the result of poor trimming—which leaves the horse more prone to harm when he steps on objects or unlevel ground—or it can be caused by a badly fitting shoe.

Treating painful sole bruising can require hoof protection, rest, and anti-inflammatory drugs for several weeks. I do not recommend

A Simple Tool for Testing Soundness

Hoof testers are a simple way to check for bruises and related sensitivity in the foot. They are large calipers used to grasp the outer wall and put pressure on the sole. Check the entire hoof with the testers, including the heels, pressing as hard as you can for 10 seconds before moving to a new spot. If a bruise (or other source of soreness) is present and causing the horse pain he will react to pressure on the affected area by flinching and pulling his hoof away.

soaking affected hooves as it will only soften and weaken the hoof. It is possible to "toughen up" the sole to help prevent bruises, and this can be achieved by painting the bottom of the foot with Venice turpentine, iodine, or an off-the-shelf "hoof freeze."

Abscesses

Occasionally, a "foreign" object works its way into the white line that attaches the sole to the wall of the hoof, the horse steps on something hard causing deep bruising, or a horseshoe nail is poorly placed, and an infection—or "abscess"—forms in the hoof. This is a very painful situation and a horse can be extremely lame as a result.

Soaking the hoof daily in a bucket of warm water and Epsom salts helps the abscess "work its way out." Hoof testers can help identify the location of the abscess, and sometimes the farrier can then dig out the infection, or part of it, with a hoof knife to reduce the pain.

Packing the hoof with Ichthammol ointment helps draw out infection.

Sometimes an abscess works its way slowly up the hoof and "erupts" at the coronary band—this is commonly referred to as a "gravel." Usually the lameness disappears when the gravel finally bursts.

Hoof Cracks

Hoof cracks are caused by trauma, conformation, or poor farrier work. Excessively dry, thin hoof walls can contribute to their formation. Commonly, cracks remain on the surface of the outer hoof wall and do not cause the horse discomfort or pain. However, if the crack extends deep enough into the sensitive inner layers of the hoof, it causes problems.

Hoof cracks generally run vertically either from the ground up, or from the coronet down—cracks beginning at the coronet tend to be more serious.

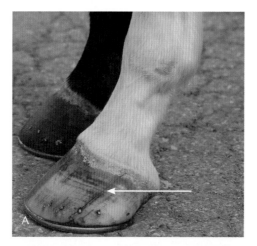

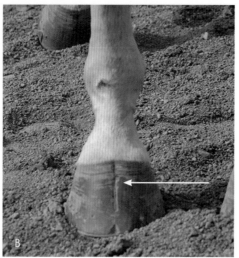

3.13 A & B Quarter crack (A) and toe crack (B)

Cracks are named according to their location on the hoof. *Quarter cracks* are the most common among Thoroughbreds because the heel quarters (the hoof wall is broken into four parts, also known as "quarters") are the thinnest part of the wall and they bear a great deal of stress (fig. 3.13 A). *Toe cracks* (sometimes called "sand cracks") are vertical cracks at the front of the hoof or toe area (fig. 3.13 B).

With correct farrier care, a lighter workload, and time, cracks eventually grow out and the new hoof wall tends to be thicker and stronger. A horse should not suffer long-term soundness issues because of a hoof crack.

Other Health Issues Coming Off the Track

Aftereffects from Anabolic Steroids

In the US, anabolic steroid use in racehorses is both legal and commonly seen. As with human use (which is *illegal* in many sporting activities), they improve the horse's appetite, stimulate production of red blood cells, promote weight and muscle gain, and speed the recovery process. Steroids are administered to colts, fillies, geldings, and mares, and can remain in the horse's system for months—consequently, negative side effects can last for a year or even longer after last administered.

The two main types of steroids used are *synthetic growth hormone* and *synthetic testosterone*, and they have slightly different effects. Growth hormone is typically used as a "finisher" for "filling out" musculature toward the end of a period of conditioning—a few weeks before racing—and testosterone is used to add aggressiveness as well as body bulk.

There are several indications of steroid use in horses:

▸ For both geldings and mares, aggressive, stallion-like behavior toward other horses is the number one sign of steroids (fig. 3.14 A). When turned out, the horse may try to mount, aggressively bite, strike, chase, or herd his pasturemates.

▸ The same aggressive streak described above may affect a gelding or mare's behavior toward his handler (fig. 3.14 B). Horses can tend to be nippy and may try to bite their handlers, and if reprimanded, they often come back fighting harder, rather than backing off.

▸ When inside, the horse may often "squeal" when other horses go by his or her stall, or at neighbors stabled next door.

▸ The horse may initially be extremely muscled through the chest, shoulders, and hindquarters, but you will notice a loss of muscle tone after steroid use has ended. Many have trouble gaining weight as their bodies adjust to the loss of muscle.

▸ Mares tend to have problems cycling. Some can only be confirmed bred after spending at least a year off steroids.

Obviously, much of the behavior related to steroid use is unappealing in horses enter-

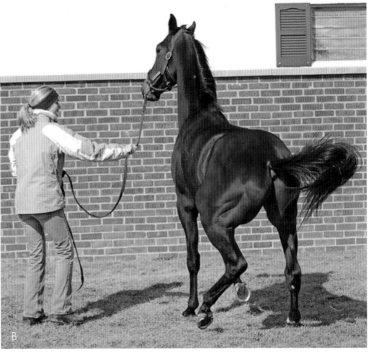

3.14 A & B Many OTTBs need time to "come down" from anabolic steroids, which are legal in US racing and can cause horses to be aggressive toward each other and difficult to handle.

ing new careers, and downright dangerous to both handlers and other horses. It is therefore important to manage the horse carefully until enough time has passed for the horse to no longer feel the steroids' effects. If you suspect your OTTB has been on anabolic steroids, there are several things that you can do to ease the transition:

1   Many horses respond well if they are quickly, but strategically, introduced to turnout. You may need to administer a mild tranquilizer for the first several sessions (ask your vet for recommendations). If possible, I recommend finding a confident yet friendly same-sex horse to turn out with your OTTB, and maintaining this single-companion set-up for several weeks, if not months, until all aggressive behavior stops.

An *extremely* aggressive horse will have to be turned out alone; again, use a mild tranquilizer if necessary at first, and remain nearby so you can make sure the horse stays relaxed and does not pace the fence line incessantly (see further discussion on p. 75).

2   If the OTTB is a gelding, I recommend keeping him stabled and pastured near other geldings, and where he cannot smell or touch a mare. Eventually, he can be introduced to mares, but wait until you are confident that he will not act aggressively. In the end, some geldings will do best if never turned out with mares.

3   Handle the horse coming off steroids as you would a stallion, and *never* take it for granted that he will not hurt you or someone else. Always use basic safety measures, such as tying the horse when grooming or working with him in the stall (see p. 96), and using a chain over his nose for leading around the barn area or to and from turnout.

4   Adjust the horse's diet as necessary, and ensure he is consuming enough calories to gain weight as he loses muscle, or he will become underweight with his ribs apparent. You can safely increase calorie content with more hay, beet pulp, and added fat.

5   Try holistic or herbal treatments that may help the horse withdraw from steroids gently—consult an herbalist or acupuncturist for his/her recommendations. At New Vocations, we use a liver flush, which seems to aid in the withdrawal process.

6   Above all, be patient and give the horse *time*. It can take a year—or even longer—for the aftereffects of discontinued steroid use to fade, and eventually disappear. The more time the steroid has to leave the body, and the longer you give the accompanying behaviors to leave the horse, the more likely you are to be satisfied with the end result.

Dealing with Gastric Ulcers

It is not uncommon for a Thoroughbred in

race training to suffer from *gastric ulcers*— erosion of the lining of the stomach due to overproduction of stomach acid. According to Dr. Nancy Loving in her book *All Horse Systems Go* (see Resources, p. 245), as many as 85 percent of racehorses examined by endoscopy of the stomach show evidence of ulcers, with their condition worsening as training progresses.

Ulcers can range from mild to severe, with the mildest case exhibiting no symptoms and more severe ulcers strongly affecting the horse's well-being, resulting in behavioral changes and a decline in physical condition and performance.

Symptoms of gastric ulcers include:

▸ Loss of appetite
▸ Change in behavior—the horse becomes grumpy or nervous
▸ Weight loss
▸ Poor hair coat
▸ Colic
▸ Decline in performance

Common factors thought to cause gastric ulcers include stress and adrenalin from competition, a heavy training schedule, change of environment or diet, long-distance transport, overuse of anti-inflammatory drugs, and lack of pasture or another source of free-choice roughage. (It has been shown that horses with access to free-choice grass or hay all day, rather than receiving only two or three measured feedings, may exhibit less of a tendency to develop gastric ulcers.)

Recommended treatments:

▸ Decreased work schedule
▸ Ample turnout, preferably with free-choice pasture
▸ Reduced stress level
▸ Ulcer medication, such as Gastrogard® or Neigh-Lox®
▸ Holistic or herbal treatments—consult a professional for recommendations

When horses first arrive at New Vocations, they often show signs indicative of gastric ulcers. However, we have found that within a week or two, most symptoms go away naturally as the horse grows accustomed to regular pasture turnout and his new environment. As I've mentioned in conjunction with other aspects of the OTTB's transition, this is one more reason why the first several weeks of life "off the track" need to be well-planned and made as free of stress as possible.

If ulcer symptoms persist in spite of changes in your horse's lifestyle then a veterinarian should step in and evaluate the horse's overall condition, including an examination of the horse's stomach with an endoscope.

Getting Your OTTB Healthy and Sound

When confronted with a lingering lameness or health issue, you will need to choose a treatment, or combination of treatments, to help ease any discomfort your horse might be experiencing and—hopefully—resolve his problem prior to launching a retraining program. There are many options available to horse owners, and it can be helpful to consult your veterinarian, as well as self-educate with books and research, in order to determine the best course of action for your OTTB.

Rest

Rest is often the very best "medicine," saving stress and expense. If possible, begin by providing your horse a safe turnout routine and just be patient!

Shoeing

As I noted earlier in this chapter, horses can retire with assorted issues related to track trimming and shoeing practices. Correcting any imbalances or other hoof issues is a necessary step in getting your OTTB healthy. Careful shoeing by a knowledgeable farrier is critical in the management of various lameness issues, as well, and it is worth remembering that corrective shoes can help alleviate many problems without resorting to more expensive treatments (see p. 102 for more on trimming and shoeing the OTTB).

Medication

It has become quite commonplace for horse owners to medicate their animals for various reasons, often with the intent to alleviate or prevent pain. Here are a few examples that are often applicable to OTTBs—either because they played a part prior to the horse's retirement from the track, or because they can help his body recover and prepare for a new career.

▶ NSAIDs (nonsteroidal anti-inflammatory drugs), such as flunixin meglumine (Banamine®) or phenylbutazone ("Bute") can be used as a temporary measure to help abate pain and aid in the healing process. However, it is important to note that high doses of NSAIDs given over a prolonged period of time may cause kidney damage, as well as ulcers.

▶ A corticosteroid (steroid) injection into veins, muscles, or joints can help alleviate swelling or inflammation for several weeks or months (corticosteroids can also be administered orally or topically, depending on the intended purpose). Long-term, high-dose use, however, has been considered a possible cause of laminitis and degeneration of bone in joints.

▶ Common joint medications, like hyaluronic acid (hyaluronan, Legend™) and polysulfated glycosaminoglycan (Adequan™), can be injected into the joint, the vein, or the muscle (depending on the product) to help improve joint fluid. In addition, there are many *oral* supplements on the market that claim beneficial effects related to joints and joint lubrication—these include methylsulfonylmethane (MSM), glucosamine, and chondroitin sulfate, as well as products containing them, among other ingredients.

Cold Therapy/Hydrotherapy

The application of cold is extremely effective for reducing inflammation and speeding healing of tendon or ligament strains, as well as joint and other leg injuries (see p. 48). This is most easily done using water (*hydrotherapy*): cold-hosing involves directing a cold stream of water at the injury for approximately 20 minutes at a time; special whirlpool boots are easier and less labor intensive than hosing; and ice buckets/boots can serve a similar function. Some commercial gels and clay poultices are also used in cold therapy.

Application is often called for several times a day, depending on your vet's recommendations.

Shock Wave Therapy

It has become popular, both on and off the track, to use the orthopedic treatment known as *extracorporeal shock wave therapy (ESWT)* to treat soft tissue and bone injuries from the outside of the horse. Short high-energy sound waves are generated (in a way similar to ultrasound) and administered to a targeted area, where they are thought to cause increased blood supply and bone metabolism. Since the procedure is noninvasive, many of the expenses and certainly the risks associated with surgery are eliminated, and it has been known to relieve injury-related pain for a short time following treatment.

Surgery

Despite the expense and lengthy recovery period, sometimes surgery is the best treatment option, especially if you're dealing with bone chips and fractures. Take this into account when you are considering purchasing or adopting an OTTB. If the candidate you are interested in may require surgical treatment, research the condition, surgery, and rehabilitation guidelines—and make sure that your bank account and your patience are up to the challenge!

Alternative Therapies

When an injury or lameness becomes chronic and fails to respond to treatments recommended by your usual veterinarian, alternative medicine or therapy can prove beneficial. Or, you may choose to explore alternative options before opting for traditional medicine or surgery. At New Vocations we have been fortunate to work with Ronald Anders, DVM, a veterinarian who also specializes in acupuncture and chiropractic. We have had

3.15 A & B Once a Thoroughbred is retired from racing, chiropractic adjustments to his neck, back, and pelvis are commonly helpful.

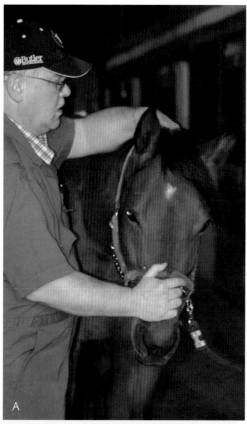

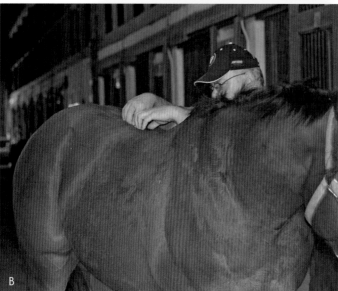

many horses with both minor and serious issues respond positively to these treatments, and others like massage.

Chiropractic

The strenuous training that racehorses have undergone often causes physical anomalies that result in discomfort in the neck, back, and pelvis. A horse that's stiff and reluctant to move forward, back up, or turn in one or both directions, may be suffering from what is called a "chiropractic subluxation," described in medical terms as "the alteration of normal dynamics, anatomical, or physiological relationship of adjacent articular (jointed) structures." In laymen's English, this means that a part of the horse's skeletal structure is partially or completely out of alignment, resulting in discomfort or pain. What starts out as a minor irritant can cause the horse to move improperly, interfering with his ability to perform and eventually developing more serious problems in other areas of his body. Plus, as a result of pain, any horse can "act out" and become difficult to handle.

According to Dr. Anders' experience with OTTBs, the following problems can potentially be resolved with chiropractic adjustment and realignment, which relieves the horse's pain at its source (figs. 3.15 A & B):

▶ Chronic lameness
▶ Neck stiffness

- Persisting back pain
- Acute and/or chronic pain in various areas of the body
- Difficulty turning, backing up, or moving forward
- Ongoing bad attitude or poor performance
- Sensitivity to head and neck handling

At New Vocations we have had many horses benefit from chiropractic treatment. I highly recommend that anyone who is working with an OTTB schedules at least one session with an equine chiropractor to help resolve many minor physical and behavioral problems that could otherwise escalate.

Acupuncture

As Dr. Anders explains, "Acupuncture can help to improve nerve and blood flow, leading to improved healing, less pain, and improved overall function of organs, muscles, and body systems." Basically, acupuncture helps the body to heal itself.

Acupuncture is an ancient practice that that has gained envious credibility in modern medicine and is becoming more and more popular in the horse world, too (fig. 3.16). I did not give acupuncture much credence until we treated several horses at New Vocations, and I was amazed by how many different problems it helped alleviate. I've witnessed it induce faster recovery from equine protozoal myelitis (EPM), lessen aggressive behavior, and reduce body soreness, to name just a few.

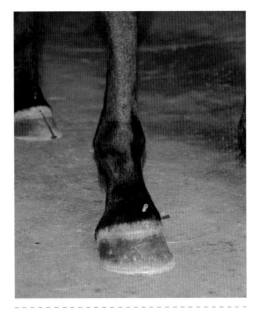

3.16 Beneficial acupuncture can be performed at points located all over the horse's body, including around the coronary band.

Some of the more common ailments successfully treated with acupuncture are:

- Poor appetite
- Prolonged diarrhea or constipation, and other issues with the digestive tract
- Chronic cough
- Neurological disorders
- Bad behavior and poor performance
- Chronic pain and stiffness in the neck and other parts of the body
- Symptoms of arthritis
- Tying-up (azoturia)
- Ovarian pain associated with heat cycles and other reproductive problems

Massage

After a long day in the saddle, you know how good a hot soak followed by a massage feels. Your horse, too, can reap the benefits of massage therapy, and today there are many qualified equine therapists offering their services throughout the US.

Thoroughbreds develop a lot of muscle soreness while training and racing, and they then re-experience this soreness as you *retrain* them for a whole new career. Massage therapy can not only help relieve any existing pain, it can prevent more pain from developing *and* help horses develop the right musculature. (Horses that aren't sore won't compensate by using the wrong muscles as they work.)

The All-Important First Step

Whatever a horse's problem and whichever treatment you decide to use, it is *imperative* that any health or soundness issues are resolved *before* you begin his retraining. In order for him to focus on the new lessons you want him to learn, he should be in the best shape possible both mentally and physically, instead of distracted by discomfort. It is well worth both time and expense to make sure that your horse is well on the road to being fit and able before you move ahead with the program.

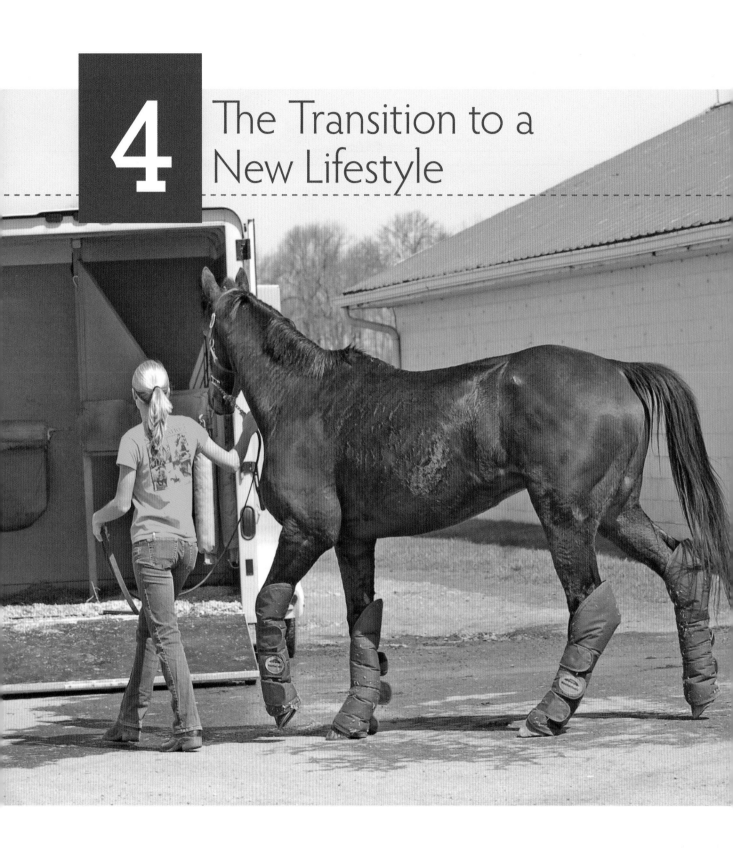

4 The Transition to a New Lifestyle

horoughbreds are bred for speed and endurance, and as I have described, their life at the racetrack is focused mainly on developing and channeling their energy for racing success (see pp. 5–27). I illustrated "life at the track" in an earlier chapter because by fully understanding what an OTTB has experienced, you can better appreciate his reaction to a new environment and training situation as he "transitions" into his career as a riding horse.

OTTBs are most vulnerable during the first couple of weeks after leaving the track and require extra patience and understanding at that time from their new owners. You must be mindful of this and never expect them to understand, without thoughtful introduction, how to behave and how to respond when new demands are placed upon them. To elaborate, the ex-racehorse will respond best when he is shown what to do step-by-step, calmly and without hurry, as many times as necessary.

In this chapter, I discuss this aspect of compassionately easing your horse into his new lifestyle. Each horse is an individual and will react as such, but there are some general steps and guidelines that will help create the least stressful transition possible. A stressed horse, just like a person, is much harder to train and connect with than one that is comfortable, relaxed, and able to focus.

Planning Ahead

Begin by planning in advance for your new horse's arrival. Before you bring him home, consider how to best provide the following:

1 A positive trailering experience
2 A welcoming and safe environment
3 A good quality feeding program
4 Confident handling
5 A tranquil introduction to turnout

Step 1: A Positive Trailering Experience

The introduction to his new home can often be impacted by the trailer- or van-ride that preceded it, so it is important to make the first transport of your OTTB's new life stress-free. When planning the event, you can, in general, safely make two assumptions:

▸ Your new horse has been hauled a lot.
▸ And, he has been hauled in taller, roomier trailers than yours.

Miles Traveled

Most ex-racehorses have had extensive experience on the road, being hauled from track to track—those that were prepped for sales were loading and traveling at a very young age, and trainers typically move to several different tracks during the season, depend-

4.1 Most OTTBs are accustomed to being hauled in open and well-lit trailers with plenty of headroom.

ing on race schedules. You can get an idea of how often a horse has traveled by examining his race record and noting how many different tracks he visited prior to retirement.

Vehicle Size

At larger tracks, trainers generally use commercial shippers, most of whom drive large, tractor-trailer-type horse vans that hold anywhere from six to 13 horses. These vans are spacious with lots of headroom and tend to have side entries that horses access via a wide ramp or a loading dock. You are more likely to see standard tag-along and gooseneck horse trailers at the smaller tracks, where trainers drive their own rigs, but even here headroom is a priority because Thoroughbreds are notorious for putting their heads straight up in the air when they are nervous.

Imagine taking a long road trip in the back seat of a cramped car, with the windows rolled up and your head pressed against the ceiling. This might give you an impression of what it is like for a horse to travel in a too-small trailer. With both your OTTB's comfort and safety in mind, arrange to use a trailer or van that is wide enough and tall enough to accommodate the horse comfortably (see fig. 4.1). At New Vocations, we require that anyone picking up a horse from our facility have a trailer that is at least 7 feet tall, and the more open and light-filled the better. We rarely have a horse that will not load into one with these dimensions.

Getting Him In, and Getting Him Home

Loading problems are usually not the horse's fault, but are caused by apprehension, which if not caused by an inadequately sized trailer, is usually the result of a previous unpleasant experience. As with any horse, an OTTB's behavior around and in horse trailers is often a direct result of: A) how he was taught to load, travel, and unload, and B) what he experienced the first few times he was transported. If a horse had a negative traveling experience when he was younger, then he will be more likely to have issues with hauling when he is older, unless someone has already taken the time to retrain him. Consider these factors the first time you move your horse, and be prepared to be infinitely patient if necessary.

Your OTTB may be quite nervous and skittish when he arrives at his new home, but don't judge his character by the way he unloads from the trailer for the first time. Some horses are more excited coming off the trailer than others, and their reactions can likely be attributed to anticipation of a new environment, a previous bad experience, or physical discomfort. Remember that when he unloads he will be surprised by his new surroundings and stimulated by them. It is important for you, or whoever is leading him to be prepared for his reactions and to remain calm, as this will encourage him to calm down, as well.

Step 2: A Welcoming and Safe Environment

At New Vocations, transitional training begins from the moment an ex-racehorse arrives. We receive, on average, two to six horses per week into the program—the majority comes directly from the track, while a small percentage comes from layup facilities or private farms where the horses may have spent up to several months. Regardless of their origins, we treat them all the same and never take their previous experiences for granted.

Most of these horses are excited and full of themselves when they step off the trailer for the first time. They look at everything, prance, nicker, and pull the handler around. While it might seem like a nice idea to lead the horse about and let him get acquainted with his new surroundings, it is generally best to take him directly to his stall to avoid him becoming even more worked up.

Stall Preparation

The horse's stall should be prepared in advance of his arrival with fresh bedding, water, and hay. It is helpful to have a horse in an adjacent stall since Thoroughbreds are as a general rule a social breed, and like most horses, tend to be happiest in the company of others. Preferably, the companion horse should be calm and steady and not the sort of animal that gets overexcited by a new arrival. This, of course, would undermine your efforts to calm down the newcomer.

Initial Anxiety

Some horses do not readily settle in to their new environment; they might pace, refuse to eat, or paw continually. There are several ways you can try to calm him. If he is pacing or pawing, "single-tying" him in the stall can help (see p. 96). Horses at the track are used to being single-tied, and he may just need someone to tell him to stand still for a while and "absorb" all the new smells, sounds, and movements.

Horses are less likely to pace or walk their stalls repeatedly when they can see what is going on around them. At the track, most horses have stall gates or webbed stall guards that allow them to put their heads out and take in their surroundings (fig. 4.2). With all the activity of life at the track, horses are kept constantly entertained. No doubt your horse will be equally interested in the activity at his new home, but bear in mind that too much excitement may increase his anxiety. Pay close attention to the amount of disruptive noise around the barn for a couple of days; the calmer the horse's environment, the calmer the horse will be. Screaming children, barking dogs, tractors, lawnmowers, or a continuous stream of visitors are only likely to get him worked up and nervous.

4.2 Usually, grooms and trainers at the track encourage their racing string to take in the surroundings by using open stall gates or web guards that allow horses to put their head out. Consider this when preparing your OTTB's new "home."

Step 3: A Good Quality Feeding Program

In general, Quarter Horses, Arabians, Warmbloods, many gaited breeds, and grade horses (among others) are much easier to maintain than Thoroughbreds, which tend to have high metabolisms that rapidly burn up calories. At the track, they are used to being fed high-energy, high-calorie grain and an unlimited amount of good-quality hay. Many people who bring home ex-racehorses have difficulty understanding and accepting how much feed it actually takes to maintain the new addition to their equine family, and frequently, an inexperienced owner cuts back a Thoroughbred's feed substantially, wrongly assuming that this will calm the "hot" horse down. Consequently, he is fed a diet deficient in calories. In my experience, it actually serves one better to give the horse all the calories his body can handle (usually in the form of fiber or fat) because not having enough to eat will only add to his being nervous and fretful.

Most horses right off the track are "race-fit," which means they are well muscled and lean with very little body fat. OTTBs quickly start to lose muscle tone when their exercise routine changes, and without sufficient grain and hay, their ribs, hips, and backbones will start to show. This can happen in as little as two to four weeks, so it is *essential* that each horse continues to receive the calories necessary to build and maintain a healthy body-weight. As the owner of an OTTB, you must pay close attention to your horse's body condition and make it a priority to help him gain fat while he is losing muscle (figs. 4.3 A & B).

Checking Body Condition

Optimal body condition can vary according to the horse's body type and activity level, but "visible" ribs or ribs that are easily felt under a winter coat are a common indicator that a horse is not receiving enough to eat. A "ribby" appearance combined with a pot belly or excessive winter hair growth is a sign of insufficient or poor quality feed, or parasite infestation. In this case, deworming is an obvious first step (you should always request information regarding the horse's regular deworming program, including dewormer type and date of last administration, prior to bringing the horse home). Then, assuming that the horse is otherwise in good health, more grain and/or additional quality hay is in order. It may take months to fatten up an ex-racehorse, but once he is in fleshy condition, the weight will be easier to maintain.

Determining Feed Type and Amount

It should not take much more than a week off the track for a horse to become accustomed to his new—and usually quite different—diet. Some horses may not want to eat much when they first arrive but eventually, their appetite should return. At New Voca-

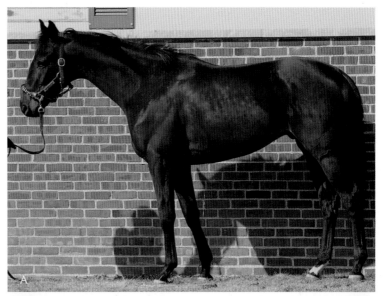

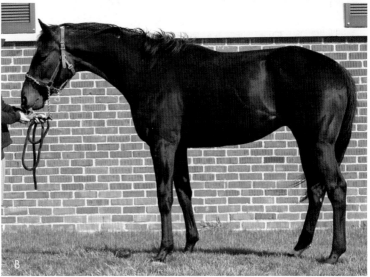

4.3 A & B A typical, race-fit, retired Thoroughbred (A), and three weeks later, when the horse has already gained weight (B).

tions we typically feed a 12 percent protein, pelleted feed along with alfalfa mix hay (see p. 73 for information on hay quality). Most horses are fed sweet feed at the track, so we often mix some of this in with the pellets to encourage newcomers to eat more readily. We hold off adding supplements until a horse is eagerly consuming his full portion of concentrated grain, and then introduce them gradually.

An OTTB needs to consume approximately 2.5 to 3 percent of his body weight in feed, of which at least 50 percent should be forage (whether grass or hay) and the rest concentrate. A baseline feeding program for an average, recently retired, 800 to 1,000 pound Thoroughbred receiving daily turnout is a total of 20 to 30 pounds of feed per day (see Weighing Feed, right). This breaks down to approximately 8 to 10 pounds of 12 percent protein concentrate, plus 12 to 20 pounds of good-quality mixed hay. Put another way, this amounts to approximately one 50-pound bag of concentrate and two-and-a-half bales of hay every five days.

For many horse owners, feeding this seemingly large amount is worrisome. If they have not owned Thoroughbreds in the past, they may be concerned that their horse will founder on a ration that includes so much grain. However, most Thoroughbreds are accustomed to eating 10 to 16 pounds of grain each day at the track. In fact, many trainers feed their horses as much as they will eat while trying to figure out how to get them to consume more! Knowing this should ease fears of overfeeding.

4.4 In the case of Thoroughbreds, it is important to accurately rate feed intake. Weighing grain can ensure you are feeding the right amount.

Weighing Feed

Weighing your horse's feed is the most accurate way to make his diet consistent. Unfortunately, many people just "guess," and due to varying levels of nutritional content or the differences in weight between corn, pelleted concentrates, sweet feed, and oats, their horses often suffer weight loss as a consequence. You should always know *exactly* how many pounds of grain and hay your horse is consuming at any time. I suggest weighing feed with a kitchen scale: first, weigh the *empty* scoop or coffee can you are using to measure the grain; then weigh the same container with the grain in it. Subtract the weight of the empty container from that of the full container to figure out the weight of the feed (fig. 4.4). To determine the weight of a hay ration, go through the same process using a hay bag.

Hay Quality and Type

Hay quality can vary greatly, depending on the time of year it was harvested, and how it has been stored. Good hay is soft, leafy, and without mold or dust.

Quality also depends on the *type* of hay you feed. Alfalfa, for example, is high in nutrient value—it has almost twice the amount of protein than timothy or grass hay—and is very palatable, so is effective for *putting weight on* horses. If you want to *maintain* your horse's weight then a good quality mix of alfalfa with orchard grass or timothy is best. If the horse is an *easy keeper*, or if he eats a lot of concentrated feed (see my earlier discussion on p. 72), straight timothy or orchard grass may be sufficient.

Note that there are always exceptions to these guidelines. When your horse is turned out on pasture with ample grass all day or all night, then hay and grain intake can be decreased; if he is fed an *unlimited* amount of good quality alfalfa, timothy, and grass hay, then often his grain intake can be decreased. The key word here is "quality." Observe your horse's weight carefully: if he starts to lose weight, increase his caloric intake with adjustments to roughage and grain amounts; if he starts to get too fat, then slowly decrease his rations. Of course, the amount of exercise that he gets will also affect your horse's weight. Don't be surprised if you need to increase his feed again when you advance his exercise program.

There has been a lot of recent research in the area of equine nutritional needs and you may be well-served by reading further on the subject (see Resources, p. 245).

Step 4: Confident Handling

Leading your OTTB out of his stall for the first time can be daunting! It is not uncommon for him to be very nervous or excited when facing his new environment. Before you embark on your first walking "adventure," consider the following:

Good versus Bad Hay

"Good" characteristics:
► Fresh, soft, with a sweet, grassy fragrance
► Palatable and easy to chew
► Alfalfa should be bright green
► Timothy, orchard grass, or Coastal Bermuda should be light green
► Oat hay (common in the Western US) should be a golden color

"Bad" characteristics:
► Dusty or moldy scent
► Yellow or brown color
► Thick, sharp, or brittle stems
► Weeds, thistle, or other debris apparent

► Horses at the track are accustomed to being led with a chain over their nose, and I find this to be the safest method when dealing with an OTTB new to me (see p. 94). Without the chain, he can pull you around or even break free—a dangerous situation for all. This does not mean that you will always need to use the chain, but while initially introducing your horse to his surroundings, it is much safer.

► Handlers at the track usually allow racehorses to walk at the speed at which they are most comfortable. This is usually a brisk walk, and the horses are rarely asked to slow down. It will be your job to teach your horse to walk at a speed that is comfortable for *you,* but this will take time. At first, respect his past experience as you ask him to manage his pace.

Common Causes of Weight Loss in OTTBs

Insufficient Calories: As mentioned earlier, if a horse is not receiving enough calories via a combination of roughage and grain, he will lose weight, especially as his "race-fit" muscling disappears. Over the years at New Vocations, I have found that insufficient feed is the number one cause of weight loss in adopted horses.

Parasite Infestation: Horses should be dewormed every 60 to 90 days, and at the track, Thoroughbreds are on a schedule to ensure this. While you should request information regarding the horse's last deworming when you buy or adopt him, it may not be available. As a precaution, it is always good to deworm a new horse to help avoid problems with condition as you begin retraining.

Heat: In a hot climate, or during the very warm seasons, a horse that spends long periods in direct sun will burn more calories than a horse that is in a stall, run-in shelter, or in the shade (see p. 84). If your horse is turned out all the time, it is important to provide him a means of shelter and shade. Inside a barn, fans can be positioned to help cool hot horses.

Cold: In regions that experience extreme cold temperatures, or during bouts of cold weather, a horse that is turned out with no shelter to protect him from wind, snow, and rain, will burn extra calories as he tries to stay warm, especially if he's wet. As in areas that experience severe heat, it is necessary to provide adequate cover from the weather. In addition, horses with thinner winter coats or those in the coldest climates may benefit from a blanket or rug.

Fighting Insects: Thoroughbreds hate insects. They tend to be thin-skinned and especially sensitive to biting flies and mosquitoes, so expect the weight to "melt" off your horse if he spends too much time fighting the bugs—inside as well as out. There are a variety of products available, including sprays, wipes, masks, and sheets, that can help keep your horse comfortable. And, scheduling turnout for the least buggy time of day is recommended.

Pacing the Fence: Running back and forth along the fence line obviously contributes to weight loss. This can be due to initial anxiety about being turned out, boredom, horses in neighboring paddocks, or a lack of company in one's own. I explain how to avoid or deal with this problem on p. 82.

Sickness: One indication of illness or disease is weight loss. Illness also weakens the horse's defenses against sudden changes in weather and parasite infestation, which contributes to the problem. If a horse is in poor condition and seems depressed, off his feed, or otherwise unwell, have your veterinarian examine him to rule out an underlying problem.

Teeth: Horses may have difficulty chewing and consequently digesting their food if teeth are sharp or in poor alignment. Watch the horse eat and note if he drops a lot of food out of his mouth while he chews. Other indicators of mouth discomfort can include issues with the bit (see p. 133), head-tossing, or poor behavior. A veterinarian or equine dentist can check your horse's teeth and "float" them—file down sharp and rough edges that may be causing problems.

► Track handlers are generally strong and confident types accustomed to handling hot young Thoroughbreds that pull on their lead rope and prance around when excited. Though, as I mentioned before, most of these handlers allow young horses to walk at their own fast pace, they do make an effort to keep the horse "on the ground and under control," since a loose horse is at risk of injuring himself, which could jeopardize his value and his racing career. Take advantage of the respect ex-racehorses have for confident handlers and move assuredly and without hesitation. Don't be afraid to remind the horse you are present and in charge should he begin to get overexcited.

I provide tips and exercises for improving ground manners and handling the horse with confidence in chapter 5, p. 94.

Step 5: A Tranquil Introduction to Turnout

After your OTTB has had his first day in his stall and has begun to acclimate to his new home, it is time to think about turnout. Remember, at the track Thoroughbreds are never turned out—they live in a stall and have no physical contact with other horses. Depending on your horse's age and history, it has therefore probably been months, or even years, since he has been outside, loose in a field with other horses—the last time was likely when he was a foal. Ideally, you will want to be able to eventually turn your horse out with company, but you need to handle this socialization with care to avoid injury and stress-related complications such as nervousness, weight loss, colic, or resurgence of ulcers (see p. 58).

Ideal Turnout Environment

Before you give your OTTB his first taste of being outside, consider the size of the turnout area. A small paddock, approximately half an acre to an acre, with secure fencing (see p. 82) is ideal. If the space is too small, the horse will have little room to escape a companion that kicks; but, too large and he has a lot of room to run, gain speed, and risk injury. The ground should be level, free of rocks and holes, and if possible, not slippery. While you may not be able to wait for a beautiful, sunny day, you should not turn your horse out in extreme weather conditions at first, especially high winds, since he will only get wound up and be more likely to hurt himself (see pp. 74 and 84 for additional information on the impact of weather on turnout).

Safety Precautions

With many a new horse at New Vocations, we use a sedative to prevent him from running himself ragged, or running into or jumping over the paddock fence. I have witnessed all

4.5 A–C When first introducing turnout to the OTTB, begin with one other horse in a small paddock. This allows him to work out any socialization issues or excess energy in a relatively small, contained space. In addition, many OTTBs benefit from a sedative, which keeps them from running or playing too hard and hurting themselves. Eventually the Thoroughbred will learn to relax and enjoy his "downtime" outside.

three of these scenarios! You can safely use a sedative for the first few days, although I don't recommend continuing use beyond one week. Speak to your veterinarian regarding your options if you feel your horse would benefit from such a precautionary measure.

In addition, you may choose to turn your horse out in protective boots or wraps to help prevent leg injuries as he grows accustomed to his freedom.

How Much Turnout?

Though it may seem like unlimited turnout is a great reward for a horse that has spent so much of his life in a stall, you should control turnout time for the first few days, at least.

In fact, a half hour may be all that a retired Thoroughbred can handle, especially if he is fresh off the track. Remember, OTTBs are most comfortable with routine and any dramatic changes in lifestyle should be made gradually.

Begin with short periods—30 to 60 minutes a day—for the first week, and see how your horse does. Some struggle with the adjustment, while others enjoy their time outside from the beginning and within days are ready to be out several hours at a time. Your goal is to incrementally increase the amount of turnout so that in one or two months, the horse can be out for up to five to ten hours, depending on your location, preference, and

facility. This amount of time will help him mentally and physically "let down."

Once the horse is comfortable outside, the longer he is turned out, the better. You know he is comfortable when he is calm and happy and maintains a good weight.

Transition to Turnout with a Herd

Introducing any new horse to a herd is similar to what a child experiences when he enters a new school halfway through the year. The horse will be scared and unsure of his surroundings, and the residents will be eager to pick on the "new kid." He will often be chased and bullied by even the meekest of the group. When the newcomer lacks confi-

dence or is very young or old, and is turned out for long periods of time in the midst of this kind of competition, then he is at risk of injury, malnutrition, or dehydration as a result. Rather than setting your ex-racehorse loose in this "pack of wolves," take things one step at a time.

The first step, which will minimize conflict and facilitate acceptance, is to turn the new horse out with one individual from the group (figs. 4.5 A–C). This should happen during the first week or two when your horse is out for short introductory periods of 30 to 60 minutes. It is best if the chosen companion is non-confrontational and naturally friendly toward other horses. Don't be surprised if they squeal, strike, or kick at each other, just be sure to monitor them, with assistance, in case the situation becomes dangerous for one of the two. At New Vocations, we see a lot of kicking out and even more squealing, yet it is rare that we have to separate horses. They normally work it out themselves and become comfortable with each other in a relatively short period of time.

The Loner

If you plan to keep your OTTB at home and you do not have other horses on your property, consider adding a companion animal to your family. This can be another horse or pony, or even a donkey or goat. In some cases, taking on a companion animal can give another retired or unwanted creature a new career, and a new life.

Horses are herd animals and do best when they have a "buddy" around to keep them company. If a companion animal is not a possibility, then boarding out may be another option preferable to keeping your horse on his own.

It is usually the new horse that will test the "boundaries" by failing to respect his pasturemate's space, which is why the first turnout "buddy" needs to be capable of politely teaching the "new guy" the rules. These two should be allowed time to bond with each other before they are introduced as a pair to another horse, or a herd. The amount of time that this requires will be determined by how quickly the OTTB adjusts to being turned out. Some horses may only need a few days

to adjust, but generally speaking between the second and fourth weeks of turnout, your horse will likely be comfortable and confident enough to move to a larger field with a group of horses.

If your facility allows, it is helpful for the new horse and his buddy to be allowed time in the "main field" while the rest of the horses are temporarily relocated. This way, when the final merger takes place, the resident horses will be entering what has now become the OTTB's territory, which will give him added confidence and bolster his image in the group.

Depending on the season, most horses will adjust to regular turnout with a herd in one to two months (fig. 4.6). At any point during the transition, if the horse seems stressed or unhappy, take a step back—shorten his length of time outside or limit the number of horses he is out with—until he is again comfortable and healthy.

His and Hers

Ideally, you have several paddocks or turnout fields to work with and can put horses together with suitable companions. Segregating mares and geldings eliminates much emotional turmoil and will lessen separation anxiety, which can become a real annoyance when you begin training your new horse. With one to three horses this may not be possible, but in larger groups it works best to have "his" and "hers" turnout areas.

4.6 Once the OTTB is comfortable in a smaller turnout area with a single buddy, then he can be introduced to a larger field with more horses.

With ex-racehorses, there is an additional issue that must be addressed: geldings that have been on anabolic steroids often exhibit stallion-like behavior for several months following the cessation of such medication (see p. 56). These horses can be self-destructive if not carefully monitored during turnout (figs. 4.8 A & B). They will often walk the fence incessantly, frantically calling to other horses, which results in weight loss and aggravation of existing or old injuries. It can help to sedate these horses each time they are turned out for several days (see p. 75). Often a gelding coming off steroids can be turned out peacefully with other geldings, but turnout with mares is out of the question. Mares should not even be in a neighboring paddock—their presence will increase the likelihood he will pace up and down the fence, put a leg through the boards, or try to jump over the fence to be with them.

I suggest putting a new horse in such a condition out with another confident gelding—one that will not feel threatened

Take the Time to Find the Right Match

At least ten horses a year are returned to our program at New Vocations because they could not "get along" with the other horses they were turned out with, or vice versa. I am always shocked when I get a phone call from an "adopter" who wants to return a horse for this reason. In our program, we work hard to put the right horses together. We frequently have a horse that doesn't like the horse or group of horses we choose for him. And, just as often, the chosen companion(s) take a dislike to the new horse. Most of the time, we give everyone a couple of days to work things out on their own. If there is no improvement in relations, then we will re-match the horses.

In the end, we have always been able to find a good match, and the process is usually easier once the new OTTB has a chance to learn some social skills. So, take time to think carefully about the situation and consider all the options available to you. If problems are related to competition over grain or hay, separate the horses while eating to limit aggression, or feed meals in stalls prior to or following turnout. Turn horses out in side-by-side paddocks rather than together—sometimes, doing this for a few days or weeks can ease initial tension before you reintroduce the pair or group. If your horse is boarded out and you have limited choices, then perhaps moving to a new facility that can better facilitate your OTTB's transition is necessary. I encourage you to be proactive in working to resolve turnout problems—don't just give up!

A

4.8 A & B When turned out next to mares, geldings coming off anabolic steroids can tend to be aggressive toward other horses or pace endlessly up and down the fence line.

B

if the new horse acts stud-like, but will put him in his place. As the steroids' side-effects wear off, the horse may be turned out with more than one gelding, but contact with mares should be avoided for at least three to six months—this "come down" time will vary depending on the amount of steroids the horse was on.

You can safely test to see if a gelding can be turned out with a mare by allowing him to touch a mare through the secure bars of a stall. If the gelding isn't particularly interested in her, you can try turning him out in a paddock next to a mare or mares, and again read his reaction. If he acts at all "studdish" when smelling a mare through the bars or over a fence, he should be kept in the company of geldings for the time being.

Additional Turnout Considerations

Fencing Type

Most Thoroughbreds have never been out in a pasture fenced with anything other than a three- or four-board vinyl or wood fencing, or woven wire with a single board on the top. High-tensile wire, cable, coated wire, tape, and electric or non-electric fencing are foreign to most of these horses (see p. 84).

Since it may be impossible to know what your horse was previously exposed to, if you have a choice, use the most visible and safe fencing available, such as wood or vinyl. If your fields are fenced with anything other than wood or vinyl, make sure to walk your horse around the perimeter before you turn him loose. If you use high-tensile wire fencing, however, don't be surprised if, once loose, he runs into or even through the fence. A "quick fix" to add visibility is to tie pieces of ribbon at intervals along the fence, which will flap in the wind and catch the horse's attention. White electric tape is a quick and affordable alternative, but it really isn't an ideal perimeter fence, since a frightened Thoroughbred still might run right through it.

Pacing the Fence

Horses pace the fence line for several different reasons (fig. 4.9). The most common cause is being turned out alone, so, as mentioned earlier, do your best to find a "buddy" for your newly retired Thoroughbred (see p. 77). Some geldings run along the fence when they can see or touch mares in the field next to them (see p. 79). We have also seen geldings that are pastured next to foals or yearlings pace the fence and even try to keep other horses away from the young herd—it seems to be an instinctual reaction, similar to what a stallion would do in the wild. The only way to solve fence-walking in these cases is to rearrange turnout areas or alternate turnout times so the horse is no longer tormented by his neighbors.

I have seen some OTTBs that were shocked by an electric fence run the fence in terror every time they are turned out. When

a horse develops this type of fear, you need to either move him to a paddock with another type of fencing, or change the fencing material in his field. While such a phobia may seem silly, it is always best to work with the horse and make his environment comfortable for him.

Not Drinking

Frequently, OTTBs do not drink when they are first turned out, either because they do not know where the water source is, or because they are afraid of the water trough. Be sure to show your new horse where the water is and that the source is safe to drink from; do not take for granted that he will

4.9 There are many reasons an OTTB may walk the fence line, often to the detriment of his health. The habit can make weight gain or maintenance almost impossible.

Feeding

OTTBs were fed in their stalls on the track, and they are not used to competing for food, so do not try to feed a recently retired racehorse outside with others. Many new aggression issues occur when food is introduced to a herd.

Also, since most OTTBs need to gain weight, it is best to feed your new horse indoors so that you know exactly how much he is eating (see more about weight gain on pp. 70–73). Not only will he likely be at the bottom of the herd's pecking order, but I've found that Thoroughbreds are often slower eaters than other horses. If your OTTB eats 9 pounds of grain and your other horse or horses eat 6 pounds of grain, chances are the Thoroughbred will never get to eat the whole 9 pounds.

Although it takes time to bring horses into the barn for mealtimes, it really is worth the effort with an OTTB. If he must eat his grain while turned out with others, choose horses that require the same amount of feed or submissive types that will not fight over food. Even then, I would recommend devising a system to separate him from his companion(s) while he is eating.

figure it out on his own or by watching another horse! It can also help to place buckets of water, like those used in his stall, near or next to the trough until he learns to drink from it.

Weather Conditions

Pay attention to weather conditions and adjust the horse's turnout schedule as necessary to keep him healthy and happy. In a hot climate, if possible, turn the horse out at night and bring him in during the day. This prevents his coat from bleaching and protects him from the heat and biting insects. In the winter, Thoroughbreds may be easily chilled, especially when they get wet, and as a result, they "shiver off" the weight that you worked hard to put on them. In colder areas it is better to turn your horse out during the day and bring him in at night when temperatures drop. In addition, blankets or rugs may be necessary (for more on this topic, see p. 74).

By considering the five steps discussed on the previous pages and planning ahead, you will be prepared to begin your horse's mental and physical transition from racehorse to riding horse. Remember, *never* take for granted that an OTTB will understand how to act in his new home. Instead, take every precaution to ensure him a gradual and safe transition. By carefully monitoring his progress and seeing that he adjusts well to each aspect of his new lifestyle before moving forward, you will establish a strong foundation upon which to build your training program.

5 Developing a Training Program

5.1

Before you begin to work your new horse it is essential that you seriously think about what you expect of his future now that you know him better. It would be ideal if there was a set training program for every Thoroughbred that retires from racing, but each horse is an individual that requires a system specifically tailored to his needs. Each horse progresses at his own rate, according to his history, temperament, intelligence, and the quality of training. Keeping this in mind, there are four questions you should ask yourself as you develop a plan:

1: What are my goals for this horse?

Earlier in this book I explained that you should have specific goals in mind when you adopt or purchase an OTTB, and with those goals in mind, you should choose a horse with the potential to perform in the discipline you are interested in pursuing (see pp. 36 and 39). Now that you have your horse home and are getting to know his personality and physical capabilities, it is time to re-examine those goals. Are they still realistic? If you took your time researching and finding the right Thoroughbred, they should be—but now they need to become more specific (for example, "I want a lower-level event horse" should evolve into "I want to compete at baby novice by the end of next year"). Break your goals down to weekly, monthly, and even yearly objectives: defining your goals will give you something to aim toward and focus on. And, identifying attainable goals as a series of stepping stones will provide the framework for a progressive training plan.

Unless you merely want to trail ride or hack out, your horse's training will eventually be geared for one discipline or another, but try to remember that not every horse fulfills his owner's initial desires: an event prospect could actually turn out to be better suited to the hunter ring if he begins to show a dislike of cross-country jumps or dressage work. An athletic horse that gets "rushy" and nervous over jumps might be happier in the dressage ring. Stay flexible and be willing to modify your plan as you go along.

2: What will this horse require to be **physically** prepared for training?

A Thoroughbred, fresh off the track, needs time to "let down" from that extremely demanding and fast-paced environment. But, contrary to what you might think, the early phase of his transition can actually be stressful

—despite the relative rest and quiet—because everything to which he is accustomed is changing. You must develop a plan to take care of his body—his *physical* needs—as it changes along with his lifestyle. So, concentrate on his nutrition, turnout schedule, shoeing program, and other aspects of his physical health (see pp. 70–85 for more detailed information). And, if the horse is recovering from an injury or illness, consult your veterinarian to ensure sufficient rehabilitation prior to beginning more serious training.

When your horse is sound, has a good appetite and a bright expression, and exhibits good body condition, then he is probably physically ready to start his new "job."

3: What will this horse require to be **mentally** prepared for training?

Your new horse will need help to *mentally* adjust to his new life, as well. When he shows signs of stress or becomes unsettled, it is your job to find ways to help him relax.

The first step is to provide a consistent, regular schedule so he feels comfortable and calm rather than anxious. Establish this with a daily routine that includes turnout time with at least one other horse (see p. 75), set feeding times that do not change erratically, and—eventually—training sessions at a regular hour of the day. If possible, it is also important to spend "other" time (the more the better) with your horse to best develop a relationship with him. Grooming and daily handling will help your horse get to know you and eventually develop a special connection with you. Thoroughbreds tend to seek human attention and form a quick bond with their handlers.

If your horse seems happy and at ease in his new home, and is no longer overwhelmed by simple tasks or fretful when tied, turned out, or being led, then his mind will likely benefit from the introduction of new stimuli via a training program.

4: Who can help me with the training process?

Turning a racehorse into a relaxed and happy riding horse is a challenging task. Unless you have a lot of experience training horses, I advise you to seek professional help, especially if this is your first time working with a horse off the track. You may not need a trainer every day, but once a week can ensure you are doing right by the horse and give you help when needed. Even if you are a professional, it never hurts to have a "set of eyes on the ground," or someone who can observe you and your horse together and make educated suggestions for improving your training program.

In today's equine industry, most trainers focus on one discipline only, such as dres-

The Five Phases of Foundation Training

Phase One

TIME NEEDED: 4 to 8 weeks

GOAL: The horse is comfortable being turned out with other horses for three to eight hours at a time. He has gained weight and his coat and hooves are in good condition. Minor aches and pains are resolved and he looks and feels good. Address any issues with his ground manners and start to develop a trusting bond by handling him and spending time with him (see p. 93).

Phase Two

TIME NEEDED: 1 to 3 weeks

GOAL: The horse halts, walks, trots, and canters calmly on the longe line or in the round pen, and is obedient to voice commands. He makes simple upward and downward transitions (walk-to-trot, trot-to-canter, canter-to-trot, trot-to-walk) and can lengthen and shorten his stride in each gait on command (see p. 109).

Phase Three

TIME NEEDED: 1 to 4 weeks

GOAL: The horse halts, walks, trots, and canters calmly on the longe line with side reins. He is willing to move forward and accept the bit, in a relaxed, balanced frame. By now you should have determined which type of bit and other equipment he works in best (see p. 133).

Phase Four

TIME NEEDED: 1 to 4 weeks

GOAL: The horse stands quietly as his rider mounts and dismounts. He halts, walks, and trots calmly under saddle in an arena or round pen (see p. 173).

Phase Five

TIME NEEDED: 1 to 4 weeks

GOAL: The horse halts, walks, trots, and canters calmly with a rider and is responsive to leg and hand aids as well as voice commands. At this point, he may be ready to go for a low-key walk outside of the arena, preferably with another horse. In addition, he is now ready to start discipline-specific training, such as jumping (see p. 205).

sage, eventing, or hunters and jumpers, so it is best to find a trainer involved in the discipline that you plan to pursue—and ideally, one who also has had experience working with ex-racehorses.

General Training Outline

Timeframe

Let's review the definition of "transition" in the context I am using the word in this book. It is the process through which something passes from one state to another. Our focus at New Vocations when "transitioning" a Thoroughbred is to help him come down from "racing mode" to a physical and mental state where he is relaxed and ready to begin his new career.

The amount of time that it takes to transition a horse from galloping at high speeds around a track to walking, trotting, and cantering calmly around an arena in a balanced manner can range from two months, to five months, or more. How long it takes to develop this *basic foundation*—something that every horse needs, regardless of your chosen discipline—depends on how well the horse responds to the initial work, as well as the overall consistency of his training. Only when this foundation is securely in place can you begin focusing on more specific riding goals (see p. 205).

In the chart on p. 89, I've laid out the OTTB's foundation training in five phases, beginning with the introduction to his new life and ending with a horse well prepared to focus on the schooling demands related to a specific discipline. Use this information as a guide only—experience will vary depending on the horse and some steps may run shorter, longer, or overlap.

6 Phase One: Starting with the Basics

Improving Ground Manners

Grooms at the track do not usually have the time to teach each horse more than the most basic of ground manners, such as standing still when being groomed and leading properly (though perhaps speedily!) Most work *around* their horses' bad habits, most notably jigging while being led, biting, kicking, or pulling back when tied. The goal is to have the horse win races, so a few stable vices are easily overlooked as long as the horse is performing well.

Try not to lose your patience when your horse exhibits some bad behavior at first. It does not mean that he will always have these habits—he has never been taught to behave any differently, most likely. I have found that many stable vices disappear soon after a horse leaves the track and adjusts to a new, more relaxed lifestyle. Many—stall weaving, for example—are developed because the horse is bored or looking for a way to use up his extra energy. So, take a lesson from the handlers on the track and plan to work around some of your horse's bad habits in the beginning. Repetitive, patient training can eventually teach him to be a pleasure to handle.

Breaking the Biting Habit

It is not unusual for an OTTB to try to bite his handler. The primary reason for this be-havior is it is a side-effect of anabolic steroid use, in both geldings and mares. Some horses that remain stallions for several years get "mouthy." Although less likely to be a reason for biting, boredom initiates many bad habits at the track, and horses like to play little "games" with those walking past their stalls (fig. 6.2). Whatever the reason, once a horse starts being mouthy, he is rarely disciplined for it—track handlers simply work around the problem.

You, however, need to stop this behavior and teach your OTTB that biting is *never* acceptable. Unlike some other common vices, it is dangerous and the horse needs to get the message that such behavior will result in a reprimand—there is nothing wrong with smacking his chest or neck with your hand or the lead rope, along with a firm verbal "No!"

There are also ways to avoid giving your horse an opportunity to bite, which can help him unlearn the habit while keeping you safe:

▶ First of all, be careful when giving treats— they can be a wonderful way to encourage your horse to look forward to seeing you, but if you always offer them from your hand, an already mouthy horse may try to bite as he looks for them. Instead of feeding them by hand, put your OTTB's treats in his feed bucket.

▶ Second, always tie a horse that bites when you are grooming him or working in his stall.

6.1 It will take time and patience to improve your OTTB's ground manners, such as standing quietly during a grooming session.

6.2 OTTBs may have bad habits, such as "making faces" or nipping at passersby. This can be due to steroid use, boredom, or simply because at the track they were never disciplined for such behavior.

Make sure the rope is short enough that he cannot reach around and bite you.

▶ Whenever handling the horse outside the stall, even just in the barn, use a chain over his nose as a teaching tool and safety device (see right). If he tries to bite you, quickly give the chain a tug as you tell him, "No!" Do this every time he tries to bite.

In addition to conscientious handling and firm reprimands when necessary, a little time as a "regular" horse will often do the trick. If you watch horses, especially geldings, turned out in a field, they often bite at each other playfully. I think that many Thoroughbreds bite out of frustration at not being able to play with other horses because I have found that OTTBs with a biting habit often stop after several weeks of turnout with pasture-mates.

Lessons in Leading

As I mentioned in chapter 4 when I discussed the significance of handling an OTTB with confidence (see p. 73), the importance of not letting your horse drag you along or walk all over you cannot be overemphasized. During early training, *every* time you lead your new horse out of his stall it is a learning experience.

Training Exercise

Choose a time to bring your horse out when the stable area is quiet—if the horse is an extremely sensitive type, make this a priority the first few times you work with him. Have an idea of the course you will follow, so you can move along confidently with a plan in mind.

I recommend using a halter and a heavy cotton lead rope with a 16-inch chain attached to the end. Thinner nylon lead ropes are harder to hold and more likely to burn your hands when the horse pulls away. Even with the cotton lead, it is a good idea to wear gloves to prevent rope burns.

Pass the chain through the near-side metal square where the noseband and cheek piece of the halter meet, wrap the chain around the noseband once, and then attach the lead snap to the halter ring under the horse's chin (fig. 6.3). When used correctly, the chain will not hurt the horse and gives you added control.

Walk on his left side, just slightly in front of his shoulder, where you have the most control (figs. 6.4 A–E). Be alert to his body language as well as any distractions around the barn area that may cause him to suddenly spook. Allow him to look around, but if he tries to pull ahead of you, maintain solid pressure on the lead and ask him to come back to your speed.

If he continues pulling forward or begins jigging, make him halt and then back up several steps to get his attention. You may have to repeat this exercise a few times until the horse relaxes and accepts his boundaries. When he walks nicely without pulling ahead, release the pressure on the lead. As soon as he speeds up, hold the lead again with steady pressure, and if necessary, stop him and back him up. Remember, *releasing* the pressure is the horse's reward for behaving well.

Practice leading him on a single route—to and from his paddock, for example—until it becomes his habit to walk quietly. If at any time he pulls forward and disrespects you, apply the pressure with the lead, halt him, and start again. If your horse simply doesn't listen and is ignoring you or running into you repeatedly, take the end of the lead rope and lightly but quickly swing it at his chest. This focuses his attention on you rather than on external distractions. While some people are uncomfortable with this course of action, it does not hurt the horse if it is done properly, but does get his attention—and it is better than being run over or dragged.

6.3 Ex-racehorses are used to being led with a chain over their nose. Continuing to use this aid will help you maintain control in new or "spooky" situations.

6.4 A–E Handle the horse from the ground with confidence. Do not allow him to lead you, but continually remind him to respect your space and pace. If he jigs or pulls ahead (B), apply pressure on the lead (C), halt him, and back him up (D). Then move forward again (E).

Eventually, most OTTBs lead quietly without a chain over the nose, especially at home. Some horses are safe without it within just a few weeks of leaving the track, while others will take much longer to understand. Even later in training, I recommend using the chain whenever you need more control, such as during a veterinary examination, when you travel to a new place, or in cold weather when horses can be "friskier."

Always act with confidence and *never* allow the horse to walk in front of you, into you, or in circles around you. If you do not deal with misbehavior and poor manners on the ground, he will grow to believe that he can get away with whatever he wants and will likely continue to push boundaries throughout the rest of his training.

Tricks to Tying

One of the most basic groundwork lessons is standing quietly when tied, whether to a single ring or on cross-ties. This is a "skill" that all horses should learn; it is essential for the handler's convenience and the safety of both horse and rider during grooming, travel, and eventually horse shows and trail rides.

Single-Tie

At the track, horses are used to being tied up in their stalls for daily grooming, tacking-up, and leg-wrapping. OTTBs are generally comfortable in the safety of their own stalls, away from distractions, so this is a good place for you to begin working with your horse on tying (fig. 6.5). In his stall, you'll need a ring or screw eye placed on the wall at least a foot

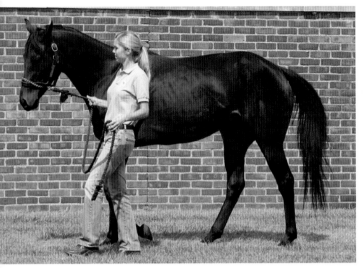

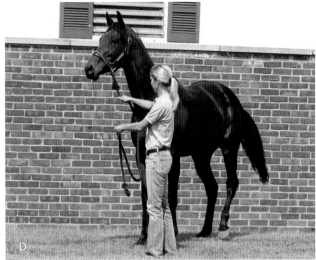

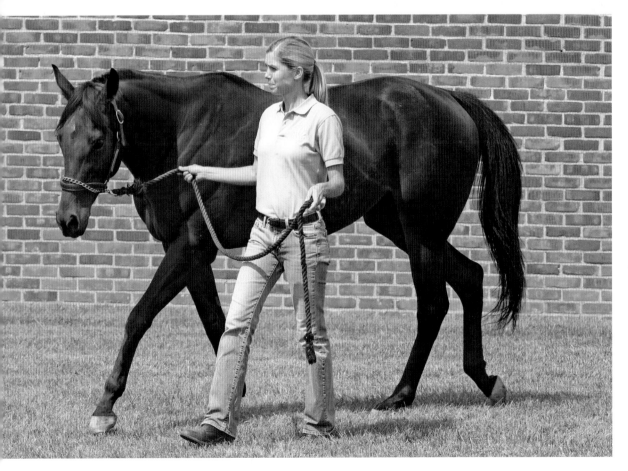

higher than his withers—anything lower and he can pull with more force and break loose, or potentially get a leg over the tie.

A tie rope made of thick rubber is a strong and flexible alternative to a cotton or nylon lead rope (www.padd-horsetack.com). *All* ties, whatever the material, should have a quick-release "safety" snap at the end to prevent the horse being injured if he pulls back hard and falls while tied. If your rope does not have a safety snap, you can create a "breakaway" device by tying a piece of baling twine to the ring or screw eye, then snap the tie or lead to the twine—it will break away easily if your horse pulls back.

When a horse habitually pulls back and breaks his halter or the stall tie, the first step in helping him overcome his fear is to determine what triggers the "flight instinct"—what makes him pull back? It could be as simple as the body brush touching a ticklish spot, or the "spray" of fly repellent, which may be new to him. Or, it could be simply an old habit that was never dealt with; horses with such problems aren't tied on the track, but simply held in place with a chain over the nose.

If you think you've identified the cause of the problem, try, for just a couple of weeks, to expose the horse to the things that seem to bother him *without* tying him. Instead, have a friend or helper hold him in his stall where he would normally be tied while you work. Then, after a few good sessions, try tying him again, but this time with a much longer tie or lead rope. It should be long enough so that the horse's hindquarters will touch the opposite wall of the stall before he comes to the end of the rope (although be sure it isn't so long that he can easily get a leg over it). In a stall of 10 by 10 feet, or 12 by 10 feet, if the horse starts to pull back, he will quickly be forced to stop by the stall wall before he can break free at his head.

Keep using the longer tie until the horse no longer attempts to pull back, then gradually shorten its length. This may not work for every horse: if the horse has been mistreated while tied in the past, his pulling back habit will take extra time and patience to overcome; and, if the horse has a chronic fear, you may not be able to tie him for months, if ever.

Cross-Ties

While it is commonplace for riding horses to stand in a barn aisle in cross-ties—two

6.6 While found in most riding stables around the country, cross-tying is not commonly seen in the shedrow. If you would like to teach your OTTB to cross-tie, begin in his stall where he is most comfortable.

him to stand quietly in them for short periods, gradually increasing the amount of time as he gains confidence. Your goal is to keep your horse comfortable and not make him feel as if he is trapped.

Once your OTTB is used to being cross-tied in his stall, then you can try to do the same in the aisle. However, some horses are never completely at ease standing in aisle cross-ties, and in those cases, you will always be safer handling them in the stall with a single-tie.

Good Grooming

Not only is regular grooming important in keeping your horse's coat healthy, but the time spent with your horse is invaluable. This interaction helps you get to know him better, and creates a bond between you. Grooming also gives you an opportunity to check your horse's legs and body for any heat, swelling, or other signs of injury or soreness, and to check the condition of his skin and coat.

Thoroughbreds at the track are usually groomed a couple of times a day: before they are worked, then again when they have dried after a bath. Grooming at the track is generally quick (but thorough), and the horse's groom usually overlooks any misbehavior as long as the job gets done.

Dealing with Misbehavior

Frequently, OTTBs dislike being groomed and show their displeasure by behaving poorly during the process. Thoroughbreds

ties affixed to either side of the aisle—most OTTBs have never been cross-tied before. If this is something you would like your OTTB to do, introduce him to the cross-ties in his stall where he is comfortable (fig. 6.6). Use loose cross-ties (outfitted with safety snaps or baling twine) at first to allow his hindquarters to touch the back of the stall if he starts to pull back, as just described. Ask

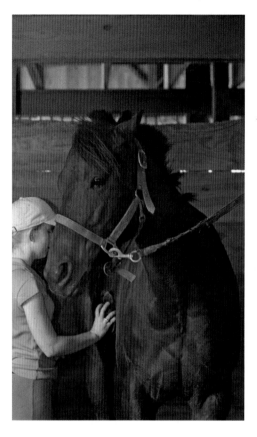

tend to have thinner, and thus more sensitive, skin than other breeds. In addition, racing can cause general body soreness, which makes being groomed an even more unpleasant experience for them. Even after leaving the track, many OTTBs still associate grooming with pain and discomfort and react in undesirable ways: pinning ears, biting the wall, lifting a hind leg, and kicking out, to name a few (fig. 6.7).

For your safety, it is a good idea to always single-tie the horse when grooming (see p. 96). This prevents him from getting his

head around to bite you or turning his hind end to kick, but you must still always pay attention to where you are standing in relation to his teeth and feet (fig. 6.8). With the horse secured, it is then up to you to work slowly and gently over his body, memorizing a "map" of his most ticklish or sore spots, and using your voice to reassure him. Keep one hand on the horse's skin while you brush with the other hand to help alleviate sensitivity and ensure he will not be surprised by "sudden" contact.

You can try to make grooming more enjoyable for your horse by using the softest brushes possible. There are some very gentle grooming products on the market, from squishy rubber "massagers" to extra-soft body brushes. Avoid metal or hard plastic curry combs and dandy brushes with stiff bristles, as they irritate sensitive skin. When your horse is really filthy or you need to remove caked-on mud, curry the worst of the mud away with a rubber curry comb and a gentle hand—or, make things easy on yourself and just give him a bath (see p. 101)!

Even when using soft brushes, some horses still react adversely to grooming. If your OTTB intensely dislikes the experience, try to find an area on his body that he enjoys having stroked or scratched. Some horses like to be rubbed on the sides of their face where the halter cheek pieces lie, or scratched in spots near their withers. You can tell if a horse is enjoying himself because he will relax by stretching his head down or leaning into the rub or scratch, as if to ask for more. Begin and end each session by brushing or scratching this "sweet spot" and he will eventually learn to enjoy, or at least *accept* being groomed.

Fly Spray

Fly spray—considered a necessity in most riding barns during certain times of the year—is actually rarely used at the track. This is because racehorses are ridden early in the morning before flies are at their worst, and stalls are cleaned twice a day with manure dispensed of far away, which minimizes flies in the stable area.

This means most OTTBs are *not* used to spray bottles—how they sound, or how liquid feels when dispensed with one. I recommend first applying fly repellent via a cloth, simply wiping it onto the horse. This will give the horse the opportunity to grow accustomed to the smell of the repellent, as well as the sound of the spray bottle as you "spritz" the cloth. When you feel your horse is ready to graduate from this initial step, have a friend or helper hold him with the chain over his nose while you stand at his side, speaking calmly to him. Begin by spraying his foreleg or shoulder lightly, and read his reaction. If he remains calm, slowly move on to the rest of his body. If the horse is still afraid, continue to use the cloth method of application, and gradually introduce the feel

6.8 For your own safety, work on grooming behavior while your horse is securely single-tied in his stall.

of the spray on different parts of his body as he grows more confident.

Bathing and Hosing

Bathing the OTTB is usually an easy task, since racehorses are bathed on a daily basis after their morning exercise. Your horse may actually enjoy being hosed down and even let you wash his face with the spray of water. However, depending on the track and trainer, the horse may be accustomed to a sponge bath and therefore be frightened of the hose. If this is the case, introduce him to hosing gradually by first directing a gentle stream of water (preferably warm) on his legs. If he remains calm, slowly move the water up his can then gradually move the stream of water up his body (fig. 6.9).

Work toward a Healthy, Balanced Hoof

During Phase One while your OTTB is acclimating to being turned out (see p. 75), gaining weight, and learning some basic ground manners, it is an opportune time to work on revitalizing his feet. If your horse's feet are not pain-free, he will not be ready for any type of training until they are. I recommend having your farrier check your horse's feet as soon as possible after he arrives, especially if he is missing a shoe or if his shoes were pulled before he came to you. This will not only allow any problems to be addressed immediately, it will also provide a basic "summary" of your horse's current hoof health, and where it needs to be.

In general, you cannot expect perfect hooves after one month's transition—it may take many months, even a year, for minor or major problems to be resolved and for new hoof to grow out, but the effort and expense spared in the long run is worth the wait.

Pulling Shoes and Reshoeing

Thoroughbreds usually race in aluminum shoes called "racing plates," which are lightweight and are not durable. Most racing plates have "toe grabs" or caulks that give the shoes greater traction and create more impulsion,

6.9 Introduce the nervous Thoroughbred to hosing by beginning with his legs, and slowly working your way up his body.

body: first on the shoulders and chest, then the neck (avoiding the head), and finally on his back and hindquarters. If he gets nervous, do not force him to endure a full bath, but just hose his legs for a short time and repeat this for a few days until he relaxes. You

A Common Skin Problem

Dermatophilosis—also known as rain rot, mud rot, or rain scald—is caused by an organism that is introduced to skin via contaminated grooming supplies, tack, or carrier flies, gnats, and mosquitoes. Horses are more susceptible to the organism when exposed to wet humid weather, wet cold weather, or when their skin has been traumatized by insect bites. In addition, it is commonly seen in racehorses because training-induced stress can weaken the immune system.

Rain rot usually presents as little bumps under the hair on the main body, though many horses also develop a form on the front surface of their lower hind legs. When closely examined, the hair may be matted with scabs on the skin; under these scabs you will find globules of pus and the infected area will be sensitive to touch.

The best form of treatment is to soften the scabs and kill the organism that caused the infection by drenching the infected area for ten minutes with an iodine-based shampoo, such as Betadine®, or a solution of iodine and warm water (Nolvasan® is also effective), then rinsing. Repeat for several days, then scrub gently to remove the scabs. Continue treatment until all the scabs are gone.

Mineral or baby oil can also be used to soften the scabs and encourage hair regrowth. With this method, you must leave the oil on the infected areas for several days before rinsing.

Do not share grooming supplies or tack between horses when one is infected, and disinfect your equipment as soon as the problem has cleared up.

translating into a faster horse. However, the same shoes that make a horse more competitive on the track place added stress on his legs.

At New Vocations we choose to leave aluminum racing plates on the front feet until the horse needs new shoes (unless, of course, the horse has an injury that can be exacerbated by caulks or toe grabs). Leaving the shoes on longer gives the hoof time to grow out so that there are fewer nail holes in the hoof when the farrier replaces the shoes. Ultimately, this makes for a stronger foot.

Toughening Up

When you want to leave a horse barefoot—either just behind or all around—try:

Venice turpentine: Painting this on is a quick way to "toughen up" sore soles and heels. You may have to apply it once or twice a day for a couple of weeks, but I've often seen results within days. This is also a good product to use when there is not enough hoof to be shod successfully and you are trying to encourage regrowth.

Hoof Freeze products: These are normally iodine-based and are used to help toughen and desensitize the horse's soles. They are used similarly to turpentine.

Hoof supplements: There are a variety of nutritional supplements that can be added to grain that are said to encourage healthy hoof growth (biotin, for example). Expect results to take 30 to 60 days, or more. Some horses benefit from being given a supplement, while others may show little change in hoof growth or quality.

Hoof conditioner: Dressings and conditioners are popular items and there are many to choose from on the market. Most intend to prevent moisture loss and therefore prevent dry, brittle hooves. I paint conditioner around the coronary band to help maintain healthy hoof growth.

We normally pull hind shoes as soon as horses arrive to reduce kicking injuries during turnout. The downside of removing these is that many horses become footsore. Thoroughbreds commonly have sensitive feet, often with thin soles and "shelly" walls that easily break or crack. Most have had shoes on constantly since they were two years old, or younger, so their feet are not tough enough to stand up to rough ground.

The Barefoot Question

While some horses have good quality feet and can be ridden and trained barefoot, many Thoroughbreds will never be entirely comfortable without shoes. Though tender feet may toughen over time (or can be helped with various products, see sidebar), I've known some broodmares that, although shoeless for years, remained footsore. You should plan on keeping your OTTB shod in front, or even all around, if you pull his racing plates and he shows signs of discomfort.

It is not uncommon for new OTTB owners to assume that their horse has a major lameness when he is actually just footsore. Hoof testers—large calipers that put pressure on the chosen area of the hoof (see p. 55)—can be used to see if the horse's soles or heels are tender. (If you don't own hoof testers, consider buying a set. They are an inexpensive investment that may save you a veterinary call.) If the horse reacts by flinching or pulling his leg away, your horse is either footsore and better off shod, or suffering from a more serious problem like an abscess (see p. 55).

You can consider leaving your OTTB barefoot when he does not test sore with hoof calipers, when you've pulled his shoes and he moves confidently and soundly (even

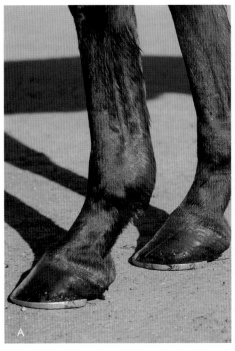

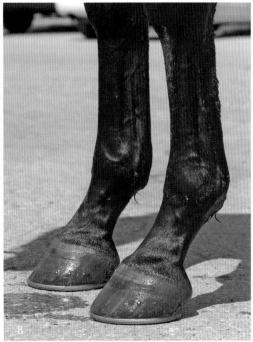

6.11 A & B Racehorses are typically shod with a low heel and a long toe (A). This offsets the optimal balance of the hoof and can lead to soundness and movement issues. Through careful, timely trimming, the heel can be allowed to grow, the toe shortened, and the hoof angle improved (B).

if there was some initial tenderness), or if there is not enough healthy hoof wall to hold a shoe. Consult your farrier when trying to determine whether barefoot is an option for your horse, or if not, which approach to shoeing would best suit his needs.

Recovering from Track Trimming

A major problem seen in OTTBs is very low or "underslung" heels. As I mentioned in chapter 3, at the track, it is a common practice to trim the heel back and leave the toe long, while general-practice farriers are trained to do the opposite (see p. 53). It is important to ascertain if your horse suffers from long toe, low heel trimming so you can immediately begin working with your farrier to correct the hoof balance (figs. 6.11 A & B). By allowing the horse's heels to grow longer, the horse will have a better base of support and correct hoof/pastern alignment, thus reducing stress on his legs and improving his way of going.

Contracted heels are often seen in conjunction with long toes and low heels—this narrowing of the foot is often a result of this type of trimming, other hoof imbalance, or poor shoeing techniques. Contracted heels limit a hoof's shock absorption qualities and can be the source of discomfort. Your farrier can promote expansion of contracted heels with proper shoeing, but it can take many months to correct.

Treating Thrush

Thrush is another common cause of sore feet in OTTBs. Bacteria in the frog of the hoof, usually resulting from poor foot or stall hygiene, cause a smelly, black discharge. This may be mildly unpleasant or, if the infection moves deep into the sensitive part of the frog, can be an outright threat to the horse's soundness.

If you suspect a thrush infection, treat it immediately. For the former, use topical medications (the "old-school" method is to paint the sole with iodine or copper sulfate, but today there are many different remedies for thrush on the market), but call a farrier to address serious cases. The farrier will cut out parts of a badly affected hoof and can suggest medicinal treatment, if necessary.

I have touched on a few of the issues most commonly seen in OTTBs; however, there are hundreds of causes of footsoreness and all manner of hoof issues that may present themselves when a horse changes careers. A good book on hoof care is an excellent investment for any horse owner, and when preparing oneself for transitioning an OTTB, it should be essential reading. I make a few recommendations on p. 246.

Moving On: When to Start Working the OTTB

When new OTTB owners ask me, "When can I start working my horse?" I tell them that there is no set answer, but to begin when their horse is both physically and mentally ready (see earlier discussion, p. 87). The horse should be allowed to "transition" at his own pace, which will vary according to the individual. Some OTTBs are ready to move on from an introductory routine of daily handling and turnout within a few weeks, while others may take several months.

I have had many horses arrive at New Vocations directly from the track that are extremely excitable for weeks, pulling handlers to and from the paddocks—often on their hind legs! Most of these horses are race-fit and may seem *physically* ready to start training as riding horses, but doing so would "blow" their minds because, obviously, they are not *mentally* prepared to handle anything new. Amazingly, after a month or two, as if a switch has been flipped, these horses usually just relax. Then, they are ready for their new work.

On the other hand, I have received horses with minds capable of quickly adjusting to life off the track that needed more time to be *physically* ready to begin work. Many have minor soreness, skin conditions, or weight issues that take a month or two to resolve.

On p. 107 I've listed what to look for when determining if your horse is both physically and mentally ready for work.

Your OTTB is *ready* to begin work when he:

- Displays a healthy appetite
- Socializes well with other horses
- Walks calmly on the lead between stall and turnout
- Sports a shiny, healthy coat
- Has strong, healthy hooves, and is properly shod (if necessary)
- Is sound (free of leg and/or body soreness)

Your OTTB is *not ready* to begin work if he:

- Does not finish his feed
- Paces the fence line and/or is antisocial when turned out with others
- Rushes to and from turnout
- Has a dull coat, rain rot, or another skin problem
- Continues to nurse tender soles or heels, or has other hoof problems
- Shows signs of body soreness
- Has an injury that has not healed

Keep these points in mind as you progress through your horse's transition. Once you feel your horse is *ready*, you can begin Phase Two: working him in a round pen or on the longe line (see p. 109). If at any point your horse regresses, demonstrating he is not ready for the new questions asked, stop and give him more time. By now, you should know him well enough to tell when he is distressed or confused. The better you come to know and understand your horse in Phase One, the better you can judge his readiness to take each new step forward in his education.

7 Phase Two: Introduction to Longeing

The Benefits of Longeing

When your horse demonstrates that he has thoroughly adjusted to his new environment and routine, he is ready to move on to Phase Two (an introduction to longeing) and Phase Three (longeing in side reins—see p. 133). *Longeing* is a method of training from the ground that allows you to put your horse through his paces without burdening him with a rider. It teaches the horse verbal cues, transitions, and balance, thus laying the foundation for future training. While some people opt to start riding their OTTBs early in their training, without much—or even any—work on the longe, I have found that the more training you do from the ground, the easier it is for you to start working with the horse under saddle. Among numerous other benefits, longeing:

► Creates a solid working relationship between horse and handler

► Encourages the horse to focus on the handler

► Teaches the horse to respond to verbal cues

► Helps the handler get to know the horse's personality

► Makes it easy to identify soreness or lameness

► Provides an effective way to introduce and evaluate new equipment

► Develops the horse's balance and ability to make transitions, and lengthen and shorten his stride

Teaching the OTTB to Longe

Some Thoroughbreds are taught to longe when they begin their race training, while others have no experience with this sort of groundwork. I recommend assuming your horse has never been longed before and starting at the beginning.

It is imperative that you teach your horse to longe one step at a time; it can take a week, or more, to teach a horse just the basics. Some, usually those with previous experience, catch on quickly, while others struggle to fully understand the concept for months. (I find that a horse that has a difficult time learning on the longe line tends to respond better to "free-longeing" in a round pen at first. See more about this option on p. 112.) You should never give in to the urge to rush through the basic steps of this kind of groundwork, as it will only result in pitfalls later on.

Two Options

There are two different approaches to teaching a horse to longe, and there are advantages to both methods:

1 The first is to start by "free-longeing" him

7.1 Longeing is a fundamental, foundational skill that OTTBs need to learn.

in a round pen and then later introduce him to work on the longe line (see below). Working the horse loose in a round pen eliminates the possibility of the horse getting tangled in the longe line or the handler getting pulled around by the horse. Off the line, the horse has more freedom to express himself and explore his own movement, which can be helpful with more difficult or energetic individuals. For new owners who have not taught a horse to longe before, this can be an easy and safe way to begin. I discuss free-longeing in detail beginning on p. 112.

2 The second way is to simply begin with the horse on the longe line. The longe line provides a direct means of communication with the horse, and when handled properly it is a safe way to reinforce verbal cues, guide the horse, and slow or stop him if he gets out of control. I generally begin horses at New Vocations on the longe line, and for experienced trainers, it may be preferable to free-longeing. I explain this process starting on p. 120.

You may choose to use both methods, or you may skip forward to longeing on the line if you do not have access to a round pen. Either way, I encourage you to read the round-penning instruction for helpful tips.

Longeing Guidelines

On the pages that follow, I've broken down my discussion into five sections:

1 Equipment
2 Environment
3 Free-longeing
4 Longeing on the line
5 Training exercise: lengthening/ shortening stride

Equipment

Whenever you work around horses you need to keep your safety, and your horse's, in mind. Both of you should be outfitted appropriately for every lesson.

The Trainer
When longeing, wear *sturdy boots* in case your feet get stepped on (remove spurs so you don't trip over them while you are standing in the middle of the longe circle), *gloves* to protect your hands from rope burns, and a *helmet* with the safety harness fastened (in case the horse kicks out). Wear a *watch* too, to make sure that you do not work the horse too long—20 minutes is plenty.

The Horse
To keep things uncomplicated, begin working the horse with minimal equipment.

▸ For free-longeing in a round pen, the horse should wear a halter and protective boots or bandages on his legs. Have a lead line or longe line, and a longe whip on hand.

▸ For work on the longe line, you can longe the horse in a halter, longe cavesson, or bridle (see p. 133 for information on choosing a bit for longe work). He should have protective boots or bandages on his legs. You will need a longe line and longe whip.

▸ Eventually, when your OTTB is confident and understands the basics of longeing, you can add a *surcingle* and *side reins* to get him used to contact with the bit, and even develop a degree of collection at walk, trot, and canter. Side reins are a safe and invaluable tool, but if you use them too soon they may frighten the horse or even cause him injury. Training must be methodical and the horse must understand what you are asking before you move on to each next step. Side reins and their uses are discussed in chapter 8, p. 133.

Environment

To be fair to the horse, you should provide him the best possible circumstances in which to learn. Choose a day with favorable weather for his first longeing experience—avoid extreme cold or heat, and especially high winds.

You need your horse's full attention, so avoid external distractions, such as tractors, lawn mowers, or other horses turned out near the round pen or longeing arena.

The round pen or arena should be enclosed by a sturdy fence at least 5 feet high. If you only have access to a large fenced-in area, be it an arena or pasture, when you practice longeing on the line, use a corner so you have a barrier on at least two sides. Especially when you first begin work with your OTTB on the longe line, the barrier can provide a much-needed sense of "containment," helping control the horse and focus his attention on you.

Your longeing space should be clear of objects such as mounting blocks, or jump poles or standards that can distract the horse and even be dangerous if he runs into them. The footing should be forgiving to the horse's legs with a solid base underneath, and it shouldn't cause slips and slides. There are many types of specialized footing available: I like dense sand with a thick clay base because the sand helps the horse gain traction and cushions each step. A grass or dirt surface can be uneven and slippery, which may cause the horse to fall or injure himself in other ways.

Note: it is necessary to maintain the footing in the round pen or arena by periodically raking the sand or other material back from the rail when it becomes banked against the sides.

The Ideal Round Pen

The best round pen for retraining an ex-racehorse is at least 50 feet, and if possible, 60 feet in diameter. This gives your horse room to walk, trot, and canter in a large circle around you while remaining close enough to heed your commands. The perimeter should be constructed of a wooden board fence (A), solid panels, or a portable steel round pen can be used, as well (B).

Free-Longeing

Though a practice long employed by horse trainers, free-longeing has gained popularity in recent times due to the general trend toward "natural horsemanship" techniques and the legion of modern trainers who have written how-to books and produced videos on round-pen work. The round pen provides an opportunity to build a trusting relationship with your horse as you start his new work experience. The more he learns to trust you, the easier it will be to introduce him to new lessons later on.

Regardless of whose techniques you choose to use—those I describe here or those of another trainer—remember that *your* goal while working your horse in a round pen is to teach him the basics of longeing in a safe and comfortable environment.

Step 1: Follow a Set Routine

As I've advised before, in order to effectively teach your OTTB a new skill, take it in stages and create a *regular routine*. The best way to do this is to work with him daily (with short, introductory sessions, the workload is not such that he needs a day off—see below), or at least three to four days *in a row* each week. Horses tend to do better if they work on consecutive days rather than every other day or on random days.

When planning how long to work your horse, remember that you want him to have a *positive*, not stressful experience, so keep the first few round pen sessions to less than 20 minutes each. Eventually, when he understands the process, you can work for a little longer—but never longer than 25 to 30 minutes. By free-longeing the horse for short periods of time, every day (see above) he will be more likely to respond to your lessons and quickly learn the new skill that you are teaching.

In addition, try to work your horse around the same time each day. I prefer this to be after a horse has been turned out, since he is more likely to focus on you once he has had a chance to run and play and get excess energy out of his system.

Step 2: Introduce the Work Area

On the first day of free-longeing, your goal should be a simple one: introduce your horse to the round pen and, if he's comfortable, begin teaching him simple voice commands (see Step 3).

This new environment is going to be his "schoolhouse"—his place of learning—so he must feel comfortable. First, lead him around the pen at the walk, letting him sniff the ground, inspect the fence, and get used to you carrying a longe whip (figs. 7.3 A–C). If he is scared of the whip, try carrying a smaller, less threatening whip such as a dressage whip, or a rolled-up longe line. The longe line can be swung in your hand and thus encourage the horse to go forward, if necessary. This also helps the horse grow accustomed to the line as part of the work environment—good preparation for later lessons.

Once the horse relaxes in the round pen, remove the lead rope and let him explore the area on his own. Stand in the center of the pen holding the longe whip with the point low to the ground, and let him walk or trot around at his leisure for a few minutes. This will encourage him to feel more independent and secure in his surroundings. Some horses adapt quickly and are content in the round pen almost immediately, while others may need a couple of sessions like this just to feel secure in the workspace.

7.3 A–C Begin by leading your horse around the perimeter of the round pen. When he seems comfortable, release him and allow him to walk or trot around quietly while you remain in the middle.

Step 3: Add Voice Commands, Body Language, and Whip Cues

Once your horse is comfortable moving about the round pen more or less on his own while you stand in the center, you can begin asking him to slow or speed up according to your verbal cues and body language (see p. 121 for more on this). Most OTTBs are not familiar with voice commands like "Walk" or "Trot," but many do respond to "clucking" and "kissing" noises, as well as the way you use your body when communicating with them. You can teach your commands of choice by incorporating cues he already knows into the lesson.

For instance, if you would like your horse to move off at the trot, say, "Trot," follow the command with a cluck, and position your body just behind the horse's shoulder, which will help drive him forward (fig. 7.4 A). The command, "Canter," would follow with a kissing cue. Eventually, he will respond to the position of your body and your first vocal command (the word), and the second vocal command (the noise) will become unnecessary.

To make downward transitions, lower the tone of your voice and drag out the vocal command—say, "Wa-a-a-alk"—and position your body "in front of" the horse's shoulder, in effect "blocking" his forward motion (fig. 7.4 B).

As you are teaching proper voice commands, you should also introduce the

> ### Dealing with Overexcitement in the Round Pen
>
> If your horse is nervous and starts racing around when you first let him loose in the round pen, drop the whip and use your body position (see below) to make him come back to you and settle. Put the horse back on the lead and walk him around the enclosure until he is again calm. If there is no obvious "external" reason for the upset, try releasing him.
>
> If the horse remains excited and again wants to run, let him do so until he is tired enough to catch him. Then, lead him around the pen several times, and finish for the day. Remember to take "baby steps" until he is focused and ready to listen.
>
> I recommend having an assistant on hand the first few times you free-longe your OTTB. A second person makes catching a frantic horse easier, and he or she can lend a hand should you need help in other ways. You may not know how your horse will react to new steps in his training, and having a friend or helper nearby is a good safety precaution.

longe whip. (If you are beginning with a dressage whip or longe line in hand instead of a longe whip, aim to gradually incorporate the standard longe whip as your horse grows more confident.) The whip should be held in the right hand when the horse is going left, and the left when he goes right, with the tip pointing toward the ground when it is not in use. When you want the horse to move from walk to trot, for example, ask by moving your body behind his shoulder and giving the verbal command. Then, if the horse does not respond, you can follow it by raising the tip of the whip to about waist level and pointing it toward his hindquarters to encourage a response.

7.4 A & B To encourage the horse to move forward or increase speed, position your body "behind" his shoulder while using your voice and whip cues, in a sense "pushing" him forward (A). To slow or stop him, move "in front of" his shoulder, "blocking" his motion and giving the appropriate verbal command (B).

How actively you use the whip depends entirely on the horse's response—if he continues to disregard the verbal command, you can swing the lash gently toward his hind end or "snap" it near the ground for emphasis. I recommend slowly incorporating more active use of the whip, as overuse in the early stages of longe training may only serve to upset or overexcite the horse (see p. 122).

Remember, your body position, voice commands, and whip aids need to work in harmony. Just like learning a new language, the key to teaching your horse verbal commands is to be consistent, correct, and repeat the process many times. If you ask exactly the same way every time, the horse will eventually understand what you want.

Step 4: Solidify Walk, Trot, and Halt

For the first several days in the round pen, stick with simple walk, trot, and halt commands. To review what I explained in Step 3: ask for trot, for example, by saying, "Trot," while at the same time moving your body behind the horse's shoulder, raising the tip of the longe whip, and clucking (subtract the "cluck" when the "Trot" command has been confirmed). When the horse responds by trotting, lower the point of the whip slightly. Remember, consistency is everything, so at first, always ask for a gait or transition in the same way.

Ideally, the horse will proceed to go around the circumference of the round pen at a medium trot. If he tries to turn into the center or move away from the rail, take a step toward him and point your whip at his hindquarters to send him forward and encourage him to stay out on the rail. The horse will not intuitively understand that he should stay close to the rail so you will probably need to correct him—patiently and frequently—in the beginning.

When making a downward transition to the walk, encourage the horse to relax and slow down by lowering the tone of your voice and positioning your body slightly in front of his shoulder. Again, the horse may want to turn into the middle of the circle. This is slightly more difficult to deal with at the walk, as moving toward him and pointing the whip could confuse him, making him think he should again trot. Therefore, during early lessons, coming into the middle after a downward transition to the walk is fine—especially if he is nervous. Just pat the horse and rub his head, neck, and body to help him relax, and then send him back out to the rail. Eventually, however, make him walk several times around the round pen after a downward transition before allowing him to stop or come in to you, or he may develop a bad habit of doing this in the middle of his lesson.

When you ask the horse for a downward transition to the halt, position your body in front of his shoulder and say, "Whoa." Many OTTBs are familiar with the "Whoa" command—they understand it means "slow down." While they may not halt immediately, you can use the word to encourage downward transitions leading eventually to a full stop. If you are consistent they will eventually "get it" and halt on the "Whoa" command.

Your horse doesn't need to stop moving for long, at first—a halt on command, however brief, deserves praise—and ask him to again move forward at the walk preferably *before* he chooses to do so on his own. Each session you can ask the horse to stand still a little longer before moving forward again, gradually working up to remaining calmly at the halt for an extended period of time.

Once your horse has grown comfortable with walk, trot, and halt commands and transitions, as well as remaining on the perimeter of the round pen, you can begin to focus on other aspects of these gaits.

Step 5: Keep His Attention and Maintain a Steady Pace

Your goal in the round pen is for your horse to respond correctly and quietly to your commands; his reaction should not be to leap forward, rush around, or ignore you altogether. The horse should only change speed, gait, or direction when you ask him (see Step 7 for more on direction). Round-pen work develops communication "patterns" and lays a foundation for the future relationship between the horse and handler. If you are lax and let the horse do "his own thing," you may well encounter problems down the road.

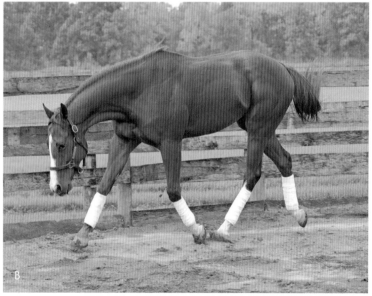

7.5 A & B If the horse appears to be slowing or growing bored with the exercise, anticipate the break into the walk by waking him up and urging him forward again into a nice, steady trot.

With this in mind, work toward keeping the horse at a *steady pace* in all gaits. Ideally, at this point you want a consistent working walk or trot that is not too slow or fast. It is often hard for an OTTB to maintain a nice working walk—many will either break into a trot or just stop—so this step alone takes a lot of discipline.

If your horse breaks gait, say from the trot to the walk, immediately send him forward in trot again. The same applies should he stop walking—send him forward again. Try to anticipate his moves and urge him forward when he slows or grows bored *before* he has a chance to break (figs. 7.5 A & B).

If your horse gets "rushy," or keeps going around and around, ignoring your command for him to slow down, walk, or halt, do not be afraid to move in front of his shoulder and place the longe whip directly in his path to help regain his attention, direct him into the rail, and make him stop. You may have to be really insistent a few times, but at this stage you want to make sure he learns to listen to you, rather than ignore you. Again, it is important to anticipate the horse's reactions, and try to change the task or lesson *before* he loses focus and gets out of control.

Step 6: Add Cantering

In the early stages of free-longeing, focus only on walk, trot, and halt. Once the horse is comfortable in both gaits and responsive to your voice commands and body language you can introduce him to canter.

Establish an easy, steady trot and ask for canter by saying, "Canter" with a cluck or "kissing" sound, moving your body behind his shoulder, and raising the tip of the whip to encourage a quick response. You want the horse to canter quietly around you in a circle without bucking, bolting, or lunging at the rail (figs. 7.6 A & B). This may not be the case the first few times you try! As soon as the horse speeds up or otherwise signals he is getting excited, ask him to come down to a trot, and then a walk. Just as at other gaits, try to read your horse's behavior and react *before* he has the chance to get over-excited.

Some horses get "fired up" in the early stages of training and will not stop running until they are exhausted and drenched in sweat. In these cases, you may want to skip cantering until you are sure he has truly mastered the downward transition to trot and walk, as well as the halt command.

Step 7: Work in Both Directions

You may find that your horse works better going in one direction over the other. All horses have one side that is stronger than the other, much like humans are right- or left-handed. I have also found that most OTTBs are more comfortable longeing to the left—not because of the direction they race on the track (see sidebar, p. 20), but because they, like many horses, are accustomed to people handling them from the left side.

7.6 A & B Encourage the horse to pick up the canter and remain on the rail without bucking, bolting, or breaking. A nice, relaxed canter will naturally help him begin to balance himself.

When starting out in the round pen, it will be easier for you to teach him voice commands and transitions when he is traveling in the direction he is most comfortable. Once he has a firm understanding of the commands and has acquired balance and steadiness at all three gaits, it will be easier for you to switch to his weaker, less comfortable side. Eventually, you want the horse to work for equal amounts of time in both directions.

Step 8: Add the Longe Line

Once your OTTB is free-longeing calmly and competently in both directions, it should be an easy transition to adding the longe line. However, it is a good idea to begin slowly as the addition of the contact of the line will feel different to your horse, and you will need to perfect this new communicative element between you.

Read through my guidelines on the next few pages before adding the longe line, and incorporate the exercise on making transitions between lengthening and shortening stride (p. 129) in your practice before moving on to Phase Three (see p. 133).

Longeing on the Line

You will not always have the luxury of a round pen in which to work your horse (or you may not have one at all), so your OTTB should be taught to behave and react appropriately to your commands on the longe line. Longeing on the line is a useful tool at any stage in your horse's training: it enables you to more easily introduce him to new equipment or new surroundings, teach him lessons before you've begun ridden work, and warm him up prior to riding. Teaching your horse to longe gives him a skill that he will most likely use for the rest of his life.

If your horse is used to working in the round pen and already responds to verbal cues, it should only take a couple of sessions for him (and you!) to become accustomed to the longe line. If you are beginning your horse's longe training on the line, rather than in the round pen, then remember to be patient and always be willing to go back a step if your horse seems to be overwhelmed by a lesson.

Longeing Techniques

If you are new to the practice of longeing, I recommend asking for help and/or instruction, or reading one of the many excellent books available on proper technique (see Resources, p. 245). Here, I touch briefly on the basic how-tos.

Using a Longe Line with a Chain

You can longe your horse in a bridle, longeing cavesson, or halter. In my experience, using a bridle too soon can frustrate the horse, as the longe line will pull on his mouth rather than his nose (see p. 133 for more about bridles).

At New Vocations, we find that most OTTBs do best beginning with a halter and a longe line that has a chain at the end, which gives the handler extra control. We use the chain until the horse is used to being longed and is less likely to pull away or disregard voice commands.

The chain is run through the inside ring of the halter and wrapped once around the noseband, then passed through the outside ring and run up along the cheek piece where it is clipped to the upper ring of the halter. Note: when you switch directions, you need to switch the chain, as well.

The handler must be very careful not to punish the horse with the chain, but only use it to apply gentle pressure when necessary, and then reward the horse by releasing that pressure.

Using a Longe Line without a Chain

If your horse is calm and responsive, or already has experience on the longe line, you can proceed to using a regular longe line without a chain, again attached to a halter, longeing cavesson, or bridle.

Without a chain, the longe line can be clipped directly to the halter ring under the horse's chin, or to the ring on the cavesson's noseband. When using a bridle, run the snap end of the line through the inside bit ring, up along the cheek piece and under the bridle's throatlatch (to secure it), then over the horse's poll, again under the throatlatch and

down along the outside cheek piece, finally attaching the snap to the outside bit ring. Note: you will need to change the line when the horse changes direction.

Alternatively, you can use a V-shaped longeing attachment or converter, which snaps to each side of the bit and has a ring for the longe line that hangs below the horse's chin. Using the attachment makes changes of direction easier and less time-consuming.

Holding the Longe Line

When the horse is traveling to the left, hold the longe line in the left hand, thumb on top, with the slack neatly folded in the right hand. Switch hands when the horse goes right (figs. 7.7 A & B). *Do not* wrap the line around either hand. The longe line extending from you to the horse should not be allowed to loop and drag on the ground—this is both unsafe and negates the ability of the line to communicate with the horse. You should keep a *steady* contact with the horse, but not a constant hard "pulling" or you will unintentionally punish him when using a chain over his nose (see p. 120), deaden his mouth if you are using a bridle and bit (see p. 133), and encourage him to lean against you.

Body Position

When working with your horse on the longe line, your body position is a useful aid. Position yourself in the middle of the circle the horse is traveling, and either walk in a small circle as

7.7 A & B Hold the longe line in your right hand, with the excess folded neatly in your left, when longeing to the right, and vice versa. The line should extend from your hand to the horse evenly and steadily, neither looping and dragging on the ground nor pulling unforgivingly on the horse's head.

you follow the horse around, or stand in one spot while pivoting around your inside foot (with a green horse you may need to walk in a bigger circle in the center to "keep with him").

Your body should generally be situated just *behind* the horse's shoulder, where you can effectively drive him forward. When asking for downward transitions, move your body *in front of* the horse's shoulder, to slow him down. Your upper body should be slightly turned in the direction that the horse is going and you should stay relaxed, with your arms at your sides and

elbows bent. Maintain a constant, soft contact with the horse via the longe line.

Longe Whip

The longe whip acts as your driving aid from the ground, as your leg does from the saddle. When longeing to the left, hold the whip in the right hand, and vice versa. The point of the whip should generally be directed down and toward the horse's inside hock, with the "thong" dragging along the ground. Raising the whip slightly should indicate to the horse that you are asking him to go forward or increase his pace, while lowering the whip slightly is the sign that you want him to slow down. Moving the whip to the opposite hand and placing it in front of the horse tells him to reduce his pace or prepares him to change direction.

Your use of the whip should depend on the horse's comfort level. Early in training, I advise against "cracking" the whip or otherwise waving it around—these actions will only scare the horse. When your horse is comfortable on the longe line, a gentle swing of the whip toward his hindquarters in order to encourage him to move forward is completely acceptable, as is a subtle "snap" down near the ground.

Commands

The verbal commands your horse should learn on the longe line include "Walk," "Trot," "Canter," and "Whoa." As I explained in the free-longeing section, OTTBs are not familiar with most verbal commands—although many do understand "Whoa"—so you will need to use a combination of body language, kissing/clucking noises, and encouragement with the longe whip in order to teach your horse to respond to them. Be consistent in how you make the commands, and use the tone of your voice to convey what you are asking. For instance, increase the tone of your voice as you ask for an increase in pace, and soften your voice when you ask him to slow down. Do not chatter incessantly or the horse will learn to ignore you. (For more about teaching verbal commands, see p. 115.)

Downward Transitions

If your horse does not know to slow down or halt with just a simple "Whoa" command, try softening your voice, lowering or even dropping the longe whip, and "giving and taking" your contact on the longe line. In the beginning, give him time to think about your request, but do not let him trot or canter endlessly around you without responding. If he still does not comply, give a couple of sharp pulls on the line and move your body in front of his shoulder to encourage him to slow down or stop. You can also point the longe whip in front of him to gain his attention (see p. 118).

Tips for Getting Started

When using a longe line you should follow the same steps as I outlined for free-longing, with some modification (see also pp. 113–119):

Step 1: Follow a set routine

Step 2: Introduce the work area

Step 3: Add verbal commands

Step 4: Solidify walk, trot, and halt

Step 5: Keep his attention and maintain a steady pace

Step 6: Add cantering

Step 7: Work In Both Directions

7.8 A–C Begin by walking the horse on the circle he is meant to travel, and gradually feed him the line as you position yourself slightly behind his shoulder to encourage forward movement. Aim to tread a small circle, or pivot, while the horse walks around you.

Getting Your Horse on the Circle

Once the horse is familiar with the work area, begin the lesson by teaching him how to work on his own on a circle.

1 Lead him in a circle the approximate size he will travel on the longe line (fig. 7.8 A). (Note: if you began with free-longeing exercises, your horse should be familiar with going on the circle.)

2 When you feel he is ready to move off on his own, drop back to his shoulder and about 2 feet from his side, keeping the line short, and pointing the longe whip toward his hindquarters to encourage him to move forward (fig. 7.8 B).

3 As the horse gets used to walking without you at his head, gradually offer him more longe line, positioning yourself just behind his shoulder and close enough to his hip to be able to drive him forward, yet far enough away so he cannot kick you (fig. 7.8 C).

4 As mentioned earlier, you may have to walk a fairly large circle with a green horse at first, but slowly work toward pivoting in the center while he circles around you.

If the horse stops and turns toward you at any time during the process, shorten the longe line and start over from the beginning.

Controlling Circle Size

During the first several sessions you may have to keep your horse on a smallish circle so that you can keep him under control. This is always preferable to allowing him to race around a larger circle before he is ready. Gradually encourage your horse to work on a larger circle as he starts to understand the basic concepts of being longed (figs. 7.9 A & B). Do this by pointing your longe whip toward his body, and giving him more longe line to encourage him to continue moving out, away from you.

It may take a while for your horse to understand you, but be consistent, and keep asking, and he will eventually figure out what you want him to do. Your goal is to work the horse out on the circle until he can work confidently with the longe line nearly completely extended. The larger the circle, the less stress placed on his legs, the more balanced he will be.

Controlling Speed

Early on, you should only teach the horse walk, trot, and halt commands, as you would with free-longeing (see p. 116). If the horse moves from halt to walk, or walk to trot, on his own, allow it for the time being as long as he keeps moving forward and does not turn and come in to you (find more about this problem on p. 117). Try to keep his focus on you and the lesson by asking him to make halt-walk-halt and walk-trot-walk transitions several times in repetition. Remember, don't be afraid to give a sharp tug on the longe line to regain his attention if he becomes distracted or speedy.

As with free-longeing, you should only allow your horse to canter once he is easily walking and trotting on a large circle and knows and respects "Whoa." If he is not ready, the request to canter may unnerve him so that he rushes, slips, and falls, or get him so keyed up he gallops around you, out of control. Do your best to keep your horse calm when teaching this new lesson. For example, if he canters and then breaks into a trot, allow him enough time to refocus and relax before you ask him to canter again—he may only canter a couple of strides before he breaks, but that is fine as long as he stays relaxed. He will be able to maintain the canter once he figures out his balance and rhythm.

If your horse does get excited and just runs around you unheedingly, use your body position, pressure on the line, verbal commands, and tone of voice to bring him back to the trot. Wait until he is quiet, and then try the canter again. Remember to take your time and don't rush the horse. Eventually your patience and consistency will pay off and your OTTB will be able to maintain a steady working canter on the longe line (figs. 7.10 A & B).

Making Direction Easy

As I pointed out earlier (p. 119), I have

7.9 A & B Keep the horse on a smaller circle early in your work on the longe, and gradually increase the size of the circle as he begins to understand what you are asking of him.

7.10 A & B Your OTTB may race around you when he begins cantering—this is generally because he is excited, nervous, or unbalanced. Stay calm and work to get a slower, more controlled canter.

7.11 A & B Many ex-racehorses find it more difficult to longe to the right than to the left. Instead of pressing the issue, wait until the horse is extremely comfortable going to the left in all gaits, and only then switch direction. Begin as you did to the left, walking him on the circle and gradually letting him go out on his own.

found that most OTTBs find it more difficult to longe to the right than to the left. I feel that this is related to their being led and handled primarily from the left side; many of them will not even lead well from the right. If this is true for your horse begin by working him on the longe line to the left, and only ask him to go right when he is competent and comfortable to the left (figs. 7.11 A & B).

Training Exercise: Lengthening/ Shortening Stride

Once your horse is comfortable walking, trotting, and cantering in both directions, either loose in the round pen or on the longe line, you can introduce a simple exercise for *lengthening* and *shortening* his stride. Lengthening and shortening his stride will loosen the horse's back muscles and strengthen his hindquarters, making him more flexible and powerful.

Note: I recommend doing this exercise on the longe line, as it gives you more control of the size of the longeing circle. However, if you have a very responsive, engaged horse, you may be able to use your body language to dictate circle size in the round pen.

1 Start at the trot on a medium-sized longe circle, slightly inside the perimeter of the round pen track or the largest circle the longe line allows.

2 When your horse has established a steady, working trot, encourage him to slightly increase his speed, driving him forward with your body language, voice, and the longe whip, as you send him out on a bigger circle. As he moves more forward on the bigger circle he will naturally start to lengthen his stride (figs. 7.12 A & B). In order to remind the horse not to break into a canter you may have to keep repeating the "Trot!" command in a steady tone. (Note: on the longe line, you may have to walk around an inner circle yourself, in order to extend the longe circle and give him more room to move.)

3 Allow the horse to trot around the larger circle several times, then use your body language and voice (and the longe line, if you are using one) to bring him in to you on a circle slightly smaller than where you began. As you do, use your "Whoa" tone of voice as you ask him to slow down and shorten his stride with "Easy," or "Slowly." The combination of the small circle and your calming tone will encourage him to shorten his stride.

Repeat the exercise several times, transitioning between lengthening and shortening, and always allowing him to go on a larger circle to lengthen his stride and a smaller one to shorten his stride. The first times you try this exercise the horse may just go faster or slower and only lengthen/shorten his stride slightly. But by changing the size of the circle and asking for a certain speed your horse will naturally start to respond by shortening and lengthening his stride on demand while maintaining a steady pace. Once he is competent at the trot, try lengthening and shortening his stride at the canter.

Reaping the Benefits

You can accomplish a lot with your horse on the longe line, so it is worth taking the time to teach him to longe correctly. By its very nature, longeing requires that you watch your horse's every move, so pay attention to how he responds to you and your commands and his environment. Though making your horse go round and round in a circle may seem simple and even redundant, if properly employed as part of your horse's training program, basic longe work can help establish a good foundation before you move on to the more advanced exercises explained in the following chapter. And, as I've said before, taking the time to work with your horse correctly and consistently from the ground will bring him one step closer to being ready to work under saddle.

7.12 A & B   Increasing the size of the longe circle will naturally encourage your horse to lengthen his stride, as shown here. Decreasing the circle, on the other hand, will teach him to shorten his stride.

Whether first free-longed in the round pen and then introduced to the longe line, or just the latter, at this point in your horse's training he should recognize and respond to verbal cues, smoothly perform transitions, and be well-balanced at all three gaits. You should be familiar enough with your horse by now to have a good idea whether or not he is ready to move on to more advanced lessons.

The next step in your horse's training is to introduce him to wearing a bridle (if you've only used a halter or cavesson until now), a surcingle, and side reins. This equipment will help you finesse the questions you ask the horse and assist you in working through any bad habits that he developed at the track, such as putting his tongue over the bit, resisting contact, tossing his head, and other evasions. Longe work in a bridle and side reins will also prepare the horse for carrying a rider since it requires that he use and develop the appropriate musculature.

There are many variations of the same equipment on the market; going to a tack store and trying to pick what is best for your horse can seem an overwhelming task! In this chapter I'll first cover the types of bits and nosebands that are most effective for use on an OTTB, and then I'll discuss how to introduce your horse to wearing a surcingle and side reins for more advanced longe work.

Bits

In order to work your horse with the surcingle and side reins you will need to use a bridle and choose an appropriate type and size of bit.

Bit Type

The majority of OTTBs have never had anything but a snaffle in their mouths; as with other horses, most racehorses are started in snaffle bits because they are the mildest type and gentle on uneducated mouths. I recommend, therefore, starting with what your horse is used to: a snaffle. Using a stronger bit at this stage will likely cause him unnecessary discomfort, confuse him, and set his training back. Later, when you have had time to gauge his response to the snaffle, you can determine if another type of bit would better suit him.

There are many different kinds of snaffle bits available. The most common are made of smooth stainless steel and are either single- or double-jointed. The single-jointed snaffle is considered the more severe of the two. When rein contact is increased, single-jointed mouthpieces have a "nutcracker" effect on the tongue and lower jaw, with the joint pressing up against the palate. Double-jointed bits adapt more readily to the shape of the horse's mouth, not pinching the tongue or poking the roof of the horse's mouth. Less commonly used are "mullen-mouthed" snaf-

8.1 Work on the longe line in a bridle and side reins prepares the OTTB's mind and muscles for carrying a rider in a new way.

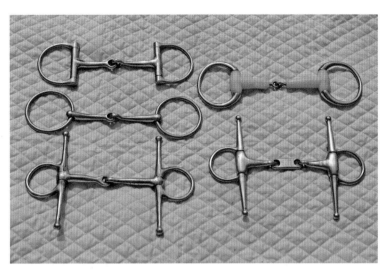

8.2 Different types of snaffles, beginning at the top left, and moving counterclockwise: D-ring, loose ring, full-cheek single- and double-jointed, and an eggbutt "Happy Mouth."

fles, which have solid, unjointed mouthpieces thought by some to be very mild, and others to be heavy and irritating to the horse due to their inflexibility.

Any variation in the snaffle mouthpiece—such as a "twist," or if the preferably smooth, rounded linkage of the double-jointed type is instead a ridge, ring, or flat plate—changes the effect of the bit. It may help to think of a smooth mouthpiece, however jointed, as the most mild, with alterations and additions to it likely adding severity. The mouthpiece can also be made of materials other than stainless steel, such as cop-

per, rubber, or flavored synthetic plastic (as in "Happy Mouth" bits), usually to promote acceptance of the bit, softness, salivation, and otherwise appeal to the horse.

Snaffles include mullen-mouthed, single- and double-jointed versions of the eggbutt, D-ring, loose ring, and full-cheek styles (fig. 8.2). People tend to prescribe to a certain cheek style for various reasons, and you may have your own favorite. I recommend beginning with the mildest style snaffle you feel comfortable with, and if your horse is unresponsive or responds adversely to it, keep trying different varieties until you find one he likes.

Snaffle Size

Bits range in width from pony-sized to draft-horse-sized. The width of bit your horse needs will depend on his facial conformation—slender muzzles need a narrower bit than less refined muzzles. Ideally, the mouthpiece should extend a quarter of an inch on either side of the horse's mouth; too wide and the bit will slide around, bruising the lips and bars, too narrow and the bit will pinch or rub the corners of the mouth, causing sores and discomfort.

Another consideration is the thickness of the mouthpiece—a horse with a small or "shallow" mouth may find a thicker mouthpiece, however smooth and mild, bulky and uncomfortable. (Note: small-mouthed horses may also be happier in a double-jointed, rather than single-jointed bit as painful pressure on their palate is more likely.) And, there are different points of potential trouble for horses with large mouths, thick tongues, or other anatomical variations (see below).

If you are inexperienced in the "art" of bitting, I recommend reading more about the pros and cons of the various snaffle types when making your choice (see Resources, p. 245). It is a complex issue and one where a little guidance can save you time and money, and spare your horse discomfort.

Dealing with Mouth and Tongue Issues

When you start working your horse in a bridle, do not be surprised if he constantly "mouths" the bit, puts his tongue over it, tosses his head, or goes around with his mouth wide open. These are all common bad habits that many OTTBs display, especially during this early stage of retraining. Many of these behaviors can be attributed to anxiety. Also, it is not unusual for racehorses to have their tongue tied down in their mouth with a strap to keep them from putting their tongue over the bit. If a horse was accustomed to having his tongue tied down whenever he was bridled at the track, he will often take advantage of his newfound freedom!

These problems can be addressed in several ways:

▸ Check Teeth

If you haven't had your horse's teeth checked by a veterinarian or horse dentist, it is always good to rule out sharp edges, wolf teeth, or other dental issues that may be causing discomfort.

▸ Wait It Out

Many horses will stop nervous habits, such as head-tossing, or mouthing or putting their tongue over the bit once they are completely relaxed, happy, and confident in a new environment. As I suggested, begin with a mild snaffle and stick with it for a couple of weeks, doing your best to ignore the problem and work on the day's lesson. Give your horse a chance to work through his anxieties before you attempt to discipline poor behavior or add tack.

▸ Change the Bit

If you have given your horse time to become comfortable in his new home with his new equipment and he continues to exhibit such behavior, try different styles of snaffle until you find one your horse likes. Often the horse is uncomfortable with a certain type or size of bit and will settle down once you find one that he likes.

▸ Adjust the Height of the Bit

Check the fit of the bit in conjunction with the bridle (figs. 8.3 A–C). Ideally, the bit should sit so there are a couple of wrinkles

8.3 A–C The bridle
should be adjusted so the
bit rests comfortably in
the horse's mouth, creating
one or two wrinkles in
the corner of his lips (A).
Too loose and it will bang
against the horse's teeth
(B), while too tight will
pull and chafe the mouth
uncomfortably (C).

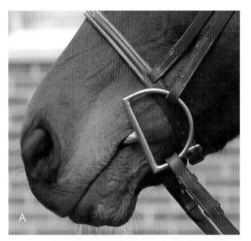

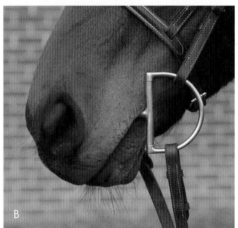

in the corners of the horse's mouth. Too low and the bit will bang against the horse's teeth—and it is easier for him to put his tongue over it. Too high and the bit will chafe and pinch the mouth, causing the horse to open his mouth or throw his head in discomfort. Bit height can be changed by adjusting the bridle cheek pieces.

If your horse has a chronic problem with putting his tongue over the bit, I have found it can help to shorten the cheek pieces of the bridle an extra hole. Once the horse realizes that he cannot get his tongue over, he will often relax, cease trying, and you can lower the bit to the appropriate height.

▸ Add a Corrective Noseband

There are several types of noseband that are useful training tools to discourage your horse from getting his tongue over the bit, opening his mouth, or crossing his jaw. These include the figure-eight (Thoroughbreds are commonly raced in this sort), flash, and drop nosebands (figs. 8.4 A–C). All three are designed to limit the amount the horse is able to open his mouth, and when correctly adjusted, they do not harm the horse or inhibit his ability to breathe or relax his jaw.

Choice of noseband will depend on A) your horse's problem; and B) your intended discipline. While your plan may be to simply use the new noseband as a training device and return to a plain cavesson when your horse has overcome his mouth and tongue issues,

 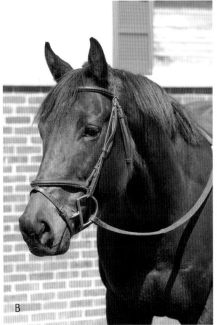 

8.4 A–C A figure-eight (A), flash (B), and drop noseband (C).

his bad habits may, in fact, continue to crop up occasionally when he feels stressed or excited. And, some horses may always need a special noseband to remind them how to behave. I have found this often relates to the age of the horse and the length of time he has gotten away with the habit—the younger the horse, and the less time he spent on the track, the more likely you will be able to correct his mouth and tongue action for good. Unfortunately, with an older horse that was raced for eight years and likes to put his tongue over the bit, chances are he will need a special noseband for the rest of his life.

If this is the case, keep in mind that some disciplines forbid the use of corrective nosebands in competition. Hunter classes, for example, only allow plain, cavesson nosebands, and dressage shows and the dressage phase at events may allow or disallow a certain kind of noseband, depending on the level of competition and other variables.

Introducing the Surcingle

Ex-racehorses are used to wearing a saddle and girth, so adjusting to a longeing surcingle with a saddle pad should not be a stressful experience. The surcingle is a band of leather or webbing that fits around the horse's back and barrel just behind the forelegs, approximately in the same place as a saddle and girth. Side reins (see below) can be attached to a series of rings at different positions on the surcingle, and then to the bit, providing a means for contact similar to a rider holding the reins.

Even though OTTBs are certainly used to being saddled, I have found that many react negatively to the process. If you watch racehorses being tacked-up in the Paddock before a race, there are always some acting up, rearing, and striking out at their handlers (fig. 8.5). These horses may be simply anticipating the race, or they may just be very sensitive to the procedure and to having the girth tightened. As you now know, poor ground manners such as this are rarely corrected at the track—trainers and grooms simply work around it.

Pay attention to your horse's reaction as you put the saddle pad on his back for the first time. This seemingly painless step can cause a horse to anticipate what comes next, and he may pin his ears or bite the wall, voicing his displeasure. Proceed calmly, but completely aware of your horse's movements as you add the surcingle, passing the straps through the girth loops on the saddle pad to keep it from slipping (fig. 8.6). A breast collar or breastplate is also helpful. I have seen surcingles used without a breast collar end up on the horse's flanks—no fun for the horse or the handler since this ticklish area will probably cause a bucking fit until the pressure is removed!

Begin by fastening the girth loosely and be prepared for the horse to act up at this point— he might rear, try to lie down, bite, kick, or strike out. Take things slowly—never tighten the girth fully in the stall, or on the cross-ties, but wait until you are in the arena before you tighten it completely. Be considerate of your horse's sensitivity and past experience, and eventually he will understand that having the surcingle tightened can be an uneventful part of his preparation for longeing.

Keep in mind that some horses buck and play on the longe because they feel frisky, but this can also be the result of sensitivity or a reaction to discomfort caused by badly fitting equipment. Since you want your horse to have a positive experience, correctly fitting, appropriate equipment is essential. If your horse is super sensitive he may benefit from using a thicker saddle pad, wither pad, and/or a fleece-lined girth or girth cover while longeing.

Work several longeing sessions in the bridle and surcingle alone, allowing your horse to become accustomed to his new "outfit" before you move on and add the side reins.

Getting Started with Side Reins

Side reins have proven to be a great teaching tool when used properly, but if used incor-

rectly they can cause further problems and undermine your efforts to instill trust in your OTTB. Before going further, you should thoroughly understand the guidelines I have provided here to ensure you use them in a way that is safe and effective.

Attached to the bit at one end and the longeing surcingle at the other, side reins simulate the rider's reins, providing consistent contact to the horse's mouth as he works on the longe line. Work in side reins accomplishes many things, among them rider, and teaching the horse to react to the bit as a *riding* horse rather than a *race*horse.

As you now know, many Thoroughbreds develop bad habits while training at the track. I mentioned some earlier (see p. 135), and "hanging on the bit" is another. An important step for your OTTB is to learn to accept pressure from the bit, and to *submit* to it, prior to your beginning work under saddle. It is instinctive for most riders to take a tighter hold on the reins when slowing or stopping a horse, but with an OTTB, this can actually make him go *faster*—jockeys tend to ride with a loose rein when they are walking or jogging, and gather their reins as they prepare for faster work (see also p. 174). Longeing in side reins helps rectify this issue before you get on board.

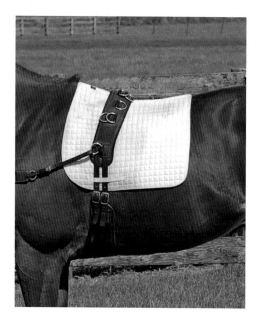

8.6 A correctly adjusted saddle pad and surcingle. Note the breast collar, which helps hold the tack in place, hooked to the lowest ring on the surcingle. To see a well-fit breast collar on the horse in motion, see figs. 8.14 A & B, pp. 150 and 151.

Early Lessons

Bring the side reins to your work area, and begin by warming up on the longe line in the bridle and surcingle (figs. 8.8 A & B). Once your horse is working well, you can add the side reins; however, if he does not relax during a warm-up *without* them, call it a day, and repeat the same introductory steps in your next session. Never push your horse too far by adding a new lesson when he is not mentally prepared

The side reins should be forgivingly adjusted the first few times you put them on the horse—just tight enough so that he knows they are there, but not enough that

providing a venue for working through the mouth and tongue issues I discussed on pp. 135–136, developing appropriate musculature for eventually carrying the weight of a

Types of Side Reins

Side reins are one of the least expensive—yet most effective—pieces of equipment used for transitioning OTTBs. There are several different types made of either leather or nylon. I prefer leather side reins as they can break easily if the horse panics and rears (thus preventing injury), while the nylon variety are unbreakable and more likely to cause a horse to flip over backward.

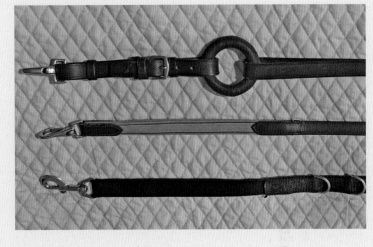

German style side reins (top) have a rubber "donut" halfway along the rein, providing a limited amount of "give." This style is best used with horses that want to hang on the bit.

Elastic side reins (middle) have a lot of "give" and are best for horses that tend to evade the bit or have extremely sensitive mouths. The elastic allows for a lighter contact, better imitating an educated rider's hands than other types.

Quick-adjustable side reins (bottom) are constructed for trainer convenience. They do not have buckles for changing rein length, but instead loop around the surcingle and snap to a series of evenly spaced D-rings, making it "easier" to shorten or lengthen them during a longeing session. If you choose to use this type, find a pair with elastic near the ends that snap to the bit, or you will find they are too restrictive for an inexperienced OTTB.

he feels restricted. If they are too short starting out, the horse could feel trapped, panic, rear, and flip over backward. I cannot stress enough the importance of starting out very *slowly* and fitting the side reins *loosely*.

Hold the side reins up against the horse to gauge the appropriate initial length (fig. 8.9). This should be determined by how the horse naturally carries his head, allowing slack when he stretches downward. If you find that

your side reins are not long enough to be fitted loosely, punch extra holes in the leather or invest in longer ones before continuing.

Once adjusted, attach the side reins one at a time—first to the rings on the surcingle and then to the bit (fig. 8.10). I prefer to use the lowest rings on the sides of the surcingle, which encourage the horse to stretch down into the contact. The upper rings better simulate the rider's hands, and can be

8.8 A & B When beginning your horse in the surcingle and side reins in the round pen, allow him time to warm up in the surcingle only. Do the same thing when starting on the longe line. Once the horse is comfortable and moving well, then add the side reins.

8.9 Always check the length of the side reins before you attach them.

8.10 When attached, the side reins should be adjusted loosely—just tight enough so the horse knows they are there, but not enough that he feels restricted.

used in later, more advanced lessons should you choose.

Place yourself in the leading position on the left side of your horse and walk him around the arena or round pen. If he does not appear to feel restricted and is comfortable walking, gradually ask him to move forward and away from you. At first, keep the longe line shorter than usual and stay several feet behind his shoulder to encourage him to continue moving forward, as the contact with his mouth may cause him to be unsure. If at any time he wants to back up or balk, return to his side and encourage him to walk next to you until he is comfortable moving forward on his own again.

When the horse seems relaxed and content, you can allow him to go on a larger circle at the walk, and then the trot. In the first several sessions, keep things simple and just walk and trot, confirming verbal commands and transitions (figs. 8.11 A–F).

Shortening the Side Reins

Keep the side reins loose until your horse is willing to walk, trot, and canter calmly in them. This generally takes about a week. Once this is achieved, you can gradually shorten them—perhaps one hole each lesson—which increases the contact with the bit and encourages him to move in a balanced frame. Use caution every time you do this: if your horse exhibits signs of panic—refusing to move, backing up, trying to rear or spin—

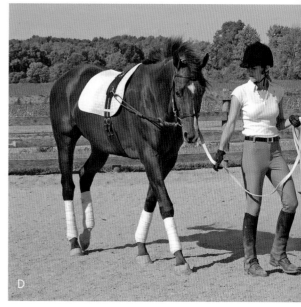

first encourage him to move forward; however, if that doesn't help, immediately loosen the side reins again to a point where he is comfortable and work him until he relaxes.

8.11 A–F In the round pen: A–C. On the longe line: D–F.

After attaching the side reins, lead your horse around the circle until he is comfortable, and stay close as you first let him out on his own. When he has adjusted to the side reins' presence at the walk, ask him to trot.

8.12 A & B If the OTTB reacts to the side reins by overflexing or carrying his head too low, move the reins from the lower D-rings on the surcingle to upper ones, and try switching to elastic side reins with more "give," as in B.

You have shortened the side reins enough when your horse is able to move forward willingly with his nose on or slightly in front of the vertical. This is the position you want him to assume for maximum physical benefit while longeing; it may only be achieved over an extended period of time. Side reins should *never* be used to crank the horse's nose toward his chest or induce manufactured flexion—even when he is physically capable of working in shorter side reins, his head should never go beyond the vertical.

Overflexion

If your horse overflexes his neck and tucks his chin to his chest then you have probably shortened the side reins too much, too soon, or the horse has a very sensitive mouth. Immediately address this problem by:

▶ Loosening the side reins to allow more freedom of movement

▶ Trying side reins that have more "give," such as the elastic type (see p. 141)

▶ Attaching the side reins to the top rings on

the surcingle, which I find encourages the horse to raise his head slightly while still giving to the bit (figs. 8.12 A & B)

▸ Changing to a different snaffle bit (see pp. 133–135)

Common Resistances Solved with Side Reins

Bear in mind, if a horse exhibits bad habits working in side reins, he will have similar problems when ridden—*unless* you take the time to work through them on the longe line before you get on his back. I've described some of the issues you are likely to encounter with an OTTB on the pages that follow.

Head-Tossing

Head-tossing is commonly seen since OTTBs often learn to fight the bit when racing. Jockeys and exercise riders generally do not try to correct this behavior, but instead simply do whatever possible to keep the horse going forward—in the end, ex-racehorses bring the habit with them when they leave the track.

8.13 A & B Head-tossing is commonly seen in OTTBs, especially when first introduced to the side reins. Encourage the horse to move forward and he will eventually relax and give in to the pressure on the bit.

If your horse tosses his head, there are several things you can do (see also p. 199). Your first task is to eliminate any dental problems. Next, ascertain whether a different size or thickness of snaffle, or a special noseband, such as a flash or figure-eight, may also help (see pps. 135–137). Finally, longeing in side reins is an excellent way to remedy this annoying habit.

Side reins provide a consistent "rein contact" with the bit, and while most horses will continue to toss their heads, or even toss their heads more often when you first begin work in side reins, work on the longe enables you to continually ask the horse to go forward when he does so, and you are therefore able to repeatedly correct the behavior. This is preferable to dealing with the issue from

the saddle, as many riders find it difficult to push the horse forward through head-tossing, and the problem only gets worse.

Start with the side reins loosely adjusted at the walk, trot, and eventually canter, and when the horse resists by tossing his head, *send him forward*. Most head-tossers are simply trying to get away from the pressure of the bit so encouraging him to move forward into the bridle will help him learn to accept it while at the same time making him work harder (figs. 8.13 A & B). It may take a week

or two but consistently reacting to the problem in this way should convince your horse that it is a lot of extra work to toss his head while moving forward.

Tense and Hollow-Backed

Thoroughbreds are a sensitive breed, prone to anxiety and tension. The racing life compounds these tendencies. A tense horse that frequently moves with his head in the air and back hollow is either experiencing pain or stiffness, or will eventually become sore and

A

a high head and a tense,
hollow back is typical
to the Thoroughbred
breed. Work in side reins
will counter this natural
inclination, encouraging
the horse to soften and
rebalance. Here, the horse
is being longed in the
round pen.

tired due to this body carriage. The use of side reins encourages him to lower his head and neck, thus bringing his back up and allowing him to "warm out of" any soreness and improve his musculature (figs. 8.14 A & B). Even just a few sessions can make a world of difference for this type of horse.

With correct training, most OTTBs can overcome this problem, although some will always start a lesson a bit tense and hollow until they've warmed-up and relaxed.

Rushing at the Canter
Some horses are perfectly comfortable mov-

B

ing on the longe at the walk and trot, but the moment they are asked to canter, they rush and become unbalanced. This is due to a couple of things. One is the horse does not yet have the muscle tone and development to work at higher speeds on a longeing circle. The second is the speed of canter most rid-ers consider a "working" canter is rarely, if ever, used at the racetrack. Exercise riders often allow the horse to begin a workout at a fast canter before bringing the horse back to a slightly slower canter for a couple of laps—and even this slower pace is much faster than that which most riders are accustomed.

This rushing issue can be a difficult problem to solve. Trot-canter-trot transitions on the longe line with side reins encourage the horse to balance himself and regulate his own speed (fig. 8.15). Focus on sustaining a relaxed and balanced trot, keeping the horse calm through the transitions, and not letting him rush forward into canter or race along at the trot after cantering. Once you begin riding the horse, you may find he still rushes at the canter despite your previous work on the longe line or in the round pen. In such cases I recommend riding him at the walk and trot *only* one day, and then working him on the longe with side reins at the trot and canter the next. Several weeks of alternating work under saddle and on the longe helps him get over the anticipation of speed that cantering once inspired and also develops his muscles and balance, thus making it easier for him to canter on a circle under a rider.

Determining When He's Ready to Ride

Most OTTBs have never been asked to move forward in side reins, so when your horse has problems understanding a new lesson, take your time and work through the is-sues, backtracking if necessary. Remember, the purpose of longeing in side reins is to produce a calm and supple horse, not an exhausted, sweaty one. Start each session without side reins and add them when the horse is relaxed. Do not drill the horse, but longe him for 20 or 30 minutes at the most, and change directions regularly so that he doesn't become one-sided. The goal is for your horse to move forward with active gaits, relax, and accept the contact with the bit.

Work in side reins should take one to four weeks, depending on the horse and how long it takes him to accept them. I also recommend adding work over ground poles to add interest to your longe lessons (see p. 209). You know your horse has developed the physical strength and mental stability to accept the rider when the horse:

- ▸ Walks, trots, canters, and halts on command on the longe in side reins
- ▸ Is willing to accept bit pressure without pulling or tossing his head
- ▸ Keeps a steady rhythm at all three gaits without stopping or rushing

8.15 During early longe training the OTTB may tend to rush at the canter—consistent, careful work in side reins, as shown here in the round pen, will help him develop muscle, balance, and the ability to regulate his own speed.

9 Making the First Ride a Success

Before you saddle up and hop on, your horse must be settled into his new management routine and working well on the longe line with side reins. With a solid foundation established through groundwork, your horse should be ready for you to begin riding him. A word of caution: if he is unsteady on the longe, or still getting used to new tack and equipment, it is best to continue working with him from the ground and resolve any problems *before* you ride.

Your horse's experience being ridden at the track is entirely different from the kind of riding that you will want to do. The purpose of exercise at the track is simply to get the horse as fit as possible and teach him to go fast—the rider is there mainly to keep the horse going in the right direction and regulate speed. So, as with every step of the training I've laid out so far, the first ride will take careful preparation.

In the pages that follow, I discuss these steps:

1 Reviewing your horse's history
2 Saddling-up
3 Preparing to mount
4 Mounting
5 In the saddle
6 Dismounting

Reviewing Your Horse's History

As with other aspects of daily life at the track, the horse's training schedule follows a strict routine. Five or six days a week, the horse is usually tacked up in his stall, then brought outside where the jockey or exercise rider is helped onto the horse's back. These riders are calm, cool customers, unfazed by jigging, scooting sideways, and other antics typical of young, fit racehorses. Skittish or young horses will often have a ground handler or "pony" rider lead them the short distance to the track and once there, turn left or right to begin their workout (see p. 20). This lasts for 20 to 25 minutes, followed by the walk back to the barn where the horse is untacked and bathed. After being walked until he is cool, probably 20 or 30 minutes, the horse is returned to his stall. Most horses are used to this routine, which is performed the same way and at the same time every day.

In addition, it is helpful to understand how racehorses are ridden. An exercise rider tends to be physically small but strong, and is used to handling skittish young horses. His focus is sending the horse on, no matter what, and while he may use a crop to encourage forward movement, he is not likely to get into a fight with a horse that is acting up. Even when the horse rears, bucks, or spooks and jumps sideways, he sticks to the saddle and continues to send the horse forward (fig. 9.2).

9.1 Make your OTTB's first experience "off the track and under saddle" a good one: plan to work in a familiar area with a capable assistant controlling him from the ground.

9.2 When a horse rears, bucks, shies, or otherwise misbehaves at the track, riders generally do not fight with or discipline the horse, but instead ride through the problem by sending him forward.

The rider either leaves the reins slack if a handler or pony rider is leading the horse, or takes a light contact with the bit. On the track, he shortens the reins, clucks or gives the horse a squeeze with his legs to ask for trot. The rider posts the trot or maintains a two-point position or "half seat," lifting himself out of the saddle with weight in the legs and the hands steady. To ask for canter, the rider (with a firm grip) shortens the reins again while giving a verbal cue and assuming—or maintaining—the two-point position. Generally, the horse responds to this shortening of the reins by moving off into the canter.

Remember that your OTTB's riding experience is probably pretty close to what I have just outlined, so at first try to follow a similar routine and ride him in a similar way, within reason. Gradually build on what he already knows and he will quickly adapt to a new way of doing things.

Saddling-Up

Plan to saddle the horse and work him on the longe line a few times before your first ride. We rarely have trouble using English saddles on OTTBs, and they seem an easy transition from practice in the surcingle (see p. 137). If you plan to retrain your horse in a Western saddle, I recommend you introduce him to the additional weight and leather gradually, adding several lessons to your training plan to allow time to do so.

The saddle you use should be in good condition and fit the horse—ill-fitting equipment that pinches or chafes will not only cause a regression in training, it can be dangerous. An experienced saddle-fitter can ascertain fit, or you can get an idea of whether a saddle is comfortable enough for your horse with a few basic checks of your own (see Resources, p. 245).

Note: as your OTTB develops musculature and adds fat, his original saddle may no longer fit him comfortably. Keep an eye on this as training progresses.

Preparing to Mount

Begin with the Familiar

Make the first ride a natural extension of a longe lesson. Work the horse in his saddle on the longe line, first warming up without side reins, then adding them so that he uses his neck and back muscles. The side reins can be attached to the girth or to the surcingle you used earlier in training (now fitted over the saddle) and clipped to the bit under the bridle rein buckle. Keep the bridle reins out of the way by undoing the throatlatch, twisting the reins several times, then threading the throatlatch through them and refastening it.

Longeing prior to mounting will enable the horse to be relaxed, supple, and ready to be ridden.

Create a Safe Environment

When you ride you should always wear a helmet with the chinstrap secured, as well as boots and gloves to ensure safety. For your first mounted sessions with your OTTB it is best not to wear spurs.

The first ride should take place in an enclosed area free of obstacles and familiar to the horse—preferably the same space you have used for groundwork. If you do not feel like it is a good day to sit on your horse—if he is tense, hot, or acting out on the longe line, a dog is barking or running underfoot, the wind is blowing, or other horses are galloping in a nearby paddock—wait for another day!

Have an Experienced Helper on Hand

Plan to have someone help you from the ground the first time you ride your horse. The handler's presence will comfort the horse and help you resist the urge to take hold of the horse's mouth if he acts up. (Note: it is *never* advisable to mount a hot, inexperienced horse without someone around to assist you.)

Further, if you plan to mount via a leg-up, you will need a second person to provide this service (see more on mounting on p. 159).

Check Your Equipment

After longeing and before you mount, remove the side reins (*never* ride with the side reins still attached). Make sure that your equipment is still correctly fit and adjusted and did not shift around during longeing. A saddle may slip around, which, if ridden in, will put uneven weight pressures on the horse's back, or it may slide too far back on to the loins and cause him to buck. Slipping back is quite commonly seen with high-withered Thoroughbreds, so as with a surcingle, it can be helpful to use a breastplate or breast collar (see p. 138). Also, be certain the saddle pad is lying flat under the saddle, the girth is in the correct place and tightened, and the leather ends of the bridle are in the appropriate "keepers" so nothing is flapping around the horse's face.

When your tack fits well and is secure, you know that any negative reactions from the horse are not the result of discomfort, but caused by something else.

Be Confident and Relaxed

Horses have the ability to sense your nervousness or tension and usually react to it. Before you get on, take a deep breath to "let go" of any anxiety. If you are unable to relax, plan to have a more experienced rider sit on your OTTB a few times until you are comfortable with how the horse behaves.

As training progresses, ideally your horse will learn to stand still as you mount, then wait calmly for your aids to move forward. But, at the track, riders often mount while the horse is moving, so the first time you get on your horse probably will not stand still.

It is imperative that you keep calm when this happens and follow the motion as he moves around. If not, he definitely will not settle and may react explosively. Tip: stay relaxed while mounting by consciously keeping your breathing calm and consistent.

Mounting

As with all aspects when training an ex-racehorse, consider the mounting procedure with which he is familiar. At the track, a handler holds the horse still or leads him at a walk as a second helper lifts the rider into the saddle. This happens either at the barn, in the Paddock, or along the path that leads to the track. The handler then continues to control the horse and the jockey or exercise rider often leaves the reins slack and his feet out of the stirrups until the horse is relatively calm (fig. 9.3, and see p. 164).

Keeping this in mind, there are two ways to mount your OTTB: getting a leg-up from a helper or using a mounting block with a ground person holding the horse. Getting on from the ground is never advised, as you will have limited control as you hop from the ground onto his back, and you put significant strain on his back as your weight pulls the saddle to the side.

Because the leg-up is the method employed at the track, it is my first choice. If you are more comfortable using a mount-

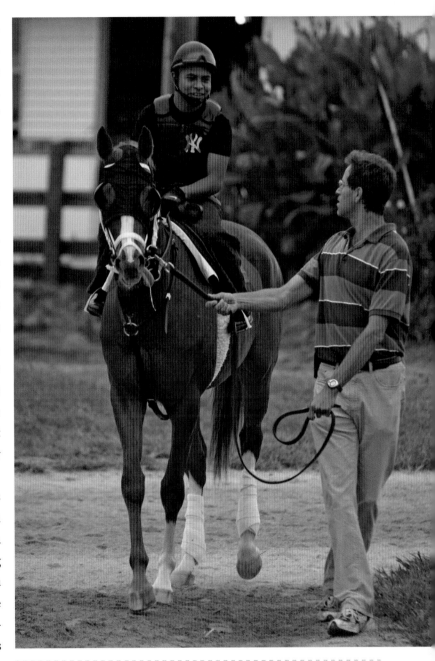

9.3 Often, an assistant controls the racehorse from the ground while the jockey or exercise rider settles into the saddle.

9.4 Do not attach the lead or longe line directly to the bit. Instead, use a V-shaped adapter or run the longe line over the horse's poll, as shown here (see Step 1).

ing block, then the horse needs to be taught to stand quietly next to the block first (see p. 161 for more on this).

Getting a Leg-Up

How-To

1 Attach the lead rope or longe line to the horse's bit via an adapter, or if using a longe line (no chain), run it through the inside bit ring and up over the poll, fastening it to the bit ring on the opposite side (fig. 9.4, and see p. 121). I do not recommend attaching the lead or longe line *directly* to the inside ring of the bit, as the handler can pull the bit right through the horse's mouth.

2 Position the horse 3 or 4 feet from the fence around the arena, facing the rail. This leaves room for him to move forward so he does not feel boxed in, but doesn't give him enough distance to get momentum if he decides to take off. The handler should stand at his head and slightly to his left side to avoid getting trampled should the horse charge forward.

3 Stand and face the horse's left side, and softly stroke his neck, back, and loins to reassure him and make him aware of your presence. Grasp the pommel of the saddle with your left hand and the cantle with the right hand and gently shift the saddle to make sure that it is settled on the horse's back and that he is comfortable with the sensation. This prepares him for movement and pressure on his back when you sit in the saddle. Take a deep breath and let it out to relax yourself and the horse (fig. 9.5 A).

4 A second helper now takes your left foot or shin in his hands as you hop slightly on your right foot while your left hand holds the reins at the withers, and your right hand grips the back of the saddle. On the count of three, the helper lifts you up and into the saddle (fig. 9.5 B).

5 As you rise, swing your right leg over the horse's back, being careful not to brush his flanks or hindquarters. Move your right

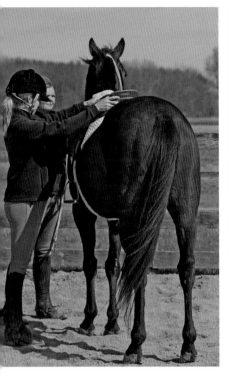

9.5 A–C OTTBs are accustomed to being mounted via a leg-up. When using this method you need two helpers on hand: one to hold the horse and another to help you into the saddle.

hand from the cantle to the horse's withers as your right leg swings over the horse (fig. 9.5 C). This should be performed quickly and cleanly, without pulling the saddle to one side. The horse should stand quietly, but if he does start to move, follow his motion and allow the movement so that he does not feel restricted or claustrophobic.

Using a Mounting Block

If you plan to use a mounting block, it should be solid and well constructed, without any gaps or protrusions that could be hazardous to the horse. It should be able to hold your weight and should not be unsteady when you stand on it. Some barns have mounting blocks fixed to the ground, which you have to position your horse next to—but in the case of retraining an ex-racehorse, a portable block is a worthwhile investment. Not only can you move it around when first introducing it to the horse (see p. 162), but you can also easily reposition it if your horse will not stand still when you try to mount. Note: buckets, muck buckets, hay and straw bales, and other objects you might use to get on a schooled riding horse are *not* suitable mounting blocks for an OTTB.

Introduce your horse to the mounting block well before you actually plan to use it. If possible, position a mounting block near the longeing area so that he gets used to it as part of his environment. Lead him up to it and let him sniff it, and have a helper hold him steady while you stand on the block beside him, without mounting. Or, place the block in the horse's paddock while he is turned out—near the gate or water trough, or in another "well traveled" area.

How-To

1 Attach the lead rope or longe line as you would preparing for a leg-up (see Step 1, p. 160).

2 Stand the horse 3 or 4 feet from the fence, facing the rail. This discourages him from bolting and encourages him to pay attention to handler and rider. The mounting block should be positioned to his left (fig. 9.6 A). Keep the situation relaxed and don't be too forceful about making the horse stand still— if he is standing next to the block and moves away, lead him calmly in a circle and stand him next to the block again. If he continually wants to move away from the mounting block, do not attempt to mount until he is willing to stand quietly.

3 As with a leg-up, the handler controls the horse as you mount. Stand next to the horse's near side, rubbing him on the neck, shoulder, and hindquarters, then step up on to the first step of the mounting block. Reassure the horse by patting him again before stepping onto the second step.

4 Grip the pommel and cantle with your hands, and slightly shift the saddle back and forth to gauge the horse's reaction to the movement (fig. 9.6 B). If he is uneasy, step down to the ground and pat him, then step back on the block. Since he will sense any tension, it is vital you are relaxed and confident.

5 Once the horse is standing quietly, and he accepts pressure and movement on his back, then you can prepare to mount. This does not mean that you should leap into the saddle straightaway! It is a good idea to test the waters by placing your hands on the saddle and your foot in the stirrup, putting just a little weight in the stirrup, then taking it away (fig. 9.6 C). (When doing this, be sure your toe does not poke the horse in his side. Some horses react strongly to this.)

6 If all seems well, again place your hands on the saddle and your left foot in the left stirrup, but now put all your weight in the stirrup and lie across the saddle (keeping your hands positioned on the saddle). Then slowly return your weight to the mounting block (fig. 9.6 D). Repeat this step several times.

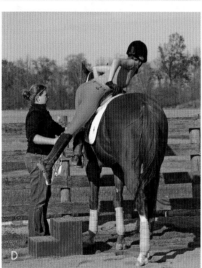

9.6 A–F Because most ex-racehorses are not used to mounting blocks—the way they look or the way you look when standing on them—it is a good idea to introduce mounting in this manner gradually, and as always, with an experienced ground person on hand.

7 If the horse remains relaxed, begin with Step 6 but this time slowly swing your right leg over the horse, being sure not to inadvertently touch or kick his flanks or hindquarters (figs. 9.6 E & F). Settle lightly into the saddle and follow the horse's motion, letting the handler take control of his head.

In the Saddle

Once you are safely on board, tell the handler to lead the horse forward. Often, just allowing the horse to move will help him calm down, whereas trying to make him stand still may only agitate him.

Taking Up the Stirrups

Leave your feet out of the stirrups at first, and let your legs hang relaxed at the horse's sides without squeezing or kicking. At the racetrack, most riders leave their feet out of the stirrups for a couple of minutes after they get on. Some even leave their feet dangling while the horse walks to the track from the stable area and *then* put their feet in the stirrups (fig. 9.7). The first few times that you sit on your OTTB, I suggest you do the same.

If the horse walks calmly (still with your feet dangling), gently press your lower legs, one at a time and then together, against the horse's sides. Do not apply too much pressure or kick him. Make sure that you warn the handler that you are about to do this so he can be prepared for the horse's reaction. A really sensitive horse might move away from one leg or bolt forward with pressure from both legs. I have found that some horses start off with *extremely* sensitive sides, but if you use the smallest amount of leg pressure at the very beginning, normally, after five minutes of walking or slowly jogging, the horse will accept gentle pressure from the leg. When

9.7 It is common practice for exercise riders and jockeys to leave their feet out of the stirrups after first mounting, and even while walking to the track.

9.8 After you have walked for about five minutes with your feet dangling and prepared your OTTB for gentle leg pressure, take up your stirrups. However, once your feet are in the stirrups, try to keep your lower leg off the horse, as shown here.

this happens, you can put your feet in the stirrups (fig. 9.8, and figs. 9.11 A & B).

There is a common misconception that the reason OTTBs have sensitive sides is because they have never felt a rider's legs. The truth is they *have* felt legs—they are just used differently than, say, a dressage rider's. Most riders who start young Thoroughbreds under saddle actually use English or Western stirrups of a normal length. And, the majority of exercise riders ride with their stirrups at a variety of lengths—for simple exercise gallops, they are usually only slightly shorter than what jumper riders might use, while timed workouts require shorter stirrups (figs. 9.9 A & B). Jockeys reserve the shortest length for actual races. Exercise riders *do* tend to grip with their knees rather than

A

9.9 A & B Exercise riders use a variety of stirrup lengths at the track. For gallops they usually ride with stirrups only slightly shorter than a jumper rider (A left & B). Timed workouts and races require shorter lengths (A right).

9.10 A & B Riders at the track tend to grip with their knees—not their seat, thighs, or legs—since they are perched over the horse's withers most of their time in the saddle (A). Keep this in mind when starting your OTTB under saddle; sit quietly with your lower leg only gently contacting the horse's sides (B).

lower legs since they perch up on the horse's withers for most of the ride, which may affect a horse's reaction to leg "grip" off the track (figs. 9.10 A & B).

Relying on Your Handler

If your horse jigs or gets nervous, be sure not to grip his sides, but focus rather on staying balanced in the saddle with only light leg pressure, patting his neck and talking to him in a calm and reassuring voice (figs. 9.11 A & B). If the horse tries to bolt forward or starts rearing or bucking, resist the temptation to grab the reins or cling with your legs. You can hold mane, the front of the saddle, or a bucking strap if you have one on; it is the handler's job to either calm the horse down or send him forward to channel his energy into something other than blowing up.

On the first day, you may find it is enough to ask the horse to walk around the ring for five or ten minutes, changing direction a few times. For a little more challenge, if you and the horse are comfortable, the handler can also longe the horse with you on his back. Begin at the walk and if that goes well, try a little trot.

- -
9.11 A & B Your assistant on the ground should be responsible for control while you prepare the horse for leg contact with your feet out of the stirrups (A). Once the horse is relaxed, take up your stirrups but resist the temptation to grip with your legs (B).

Bing's Story

I believe that some Thoroughbreds are just more sensitive than others. Take, for example, a horse named Bingalong Flight (a.k.a. "Bing") that came to our program in 2002. Having raced over 50 times, he was retired because he was no longer competitive. After a year of schooling on the flat and over fences he still remained highly sensitive to the rider's leg.

Consistent work helped him, but if Bing was given several days off or missed a couple of days of turnout, his sides would be extremely sensitive again. Longeing before riding him would occasionally help, but even so, some days we knew that he needed five to ten minutes to warm up without a lot of leg pressure from the rider. Other days any leg pressure at all would initiate a tense, over-collected canter. The thing was, we knew it wasn't due to being unaccustomed to leg pressure, because by the end of many lessons, he would actually become so dead-sided that his rider would need a crop or spurs to keep him moving forward with any energy!

I can't say for sure why Bing and others like him need extra time at the beginning of each ride to accept leg pressure against their sides. Even now he still has days when he needs extra warm-up time, and then he has others when he is receptive to the leg from the minute you get on. There are some things that you will need to accept as particular to an individual horse; it is your job as the new rider to learn how to work with, and not against, these characteristics.

You can also try walking around *without* the ground person. Don't be in a rush for independence though—the handler is your best friend at this point, and you should be content as the passenger while the horse gets used to having weight on his back again (fig. 9.12). Take your time and keep the horse in his comfort zone. You are not out to set records for the most quickly trained horse: walking around and staying calm and relaxed is a lofty enough goal at the start.

Dismounting

At the racetrack, a handler holds the horse while the jockey or exercise rider dismounts. Doing the same early on will be a comfort to your OTTB, so make sure your ground person is on hand at the end of your first few rides. This will also act as a precautionary measure in case the horse has any hang-ups with the dismounting process.

Remember, little steps still take you forward. Each time you sit on your horse—even for a few minutes—he is learning it is okay to be ridden and that he can remain calm under saddle. When you feel that he is comfortable carrying your weight and you can mount and dismount safely, it is time to move on to more challenging work.

9.12 Aim for the horse to travel quietly and become accustomed to your seat and leg pressure. A ground person should lead or longe the horse until both you and the horse are calm and in control.

Now that your horse is comfortable with you mounting and dismounting and walking with a rider up around the arena, you can move forward with his training under saddle. In this chapter, I discuss, step-by-step, the basics of riding the green OTTB. These early lessons are important because they build on the lessons he learned through groundwork and establish the foundation for your horse's later career-specific training. As you go, there will be times when he reverts to old patterns of behavior, or gets confused and misbehaves, but with plenty of patience you can stick with the program and see him through the tough times. It will be your consistent hard work that helps your horse successfully transition to his new job.

Six Tips for Under Saddle Training

By now you may feel you have spent more time thinking about your OTTB's past than you have planning his future! But, before you progress further it helps to again review how your horse was trained and managed before he came to you. Here are a few important points to keep in mind:

Stick to a Routine

As previously noted, Thoroughbreds are not only used to consistency, they tend to thrive on it. By now you should have established a schedule that your horse is comfortable with so he is able to relax and focus. His "new" ridden work should be a *natural* progression from what he has learned over the last several weeks or months since you purchased or adopted him.

Short Workouts

On the track, horses are usually only worked under saddle for about 20 to 30 minutes. I have found that early in an OTTB's retraining, it is best to ride for no more than 30 minutes at a time. Short *daily* sessions are more useful than longer sessions fewer days a week. When the horse understands the riding lessons and develops the correct muscles, you can increase his work time.

Warm Up and Cool Down

Longe the horse quietly for five to ten minutes to warm up before you ride. It's a good time, as he trots around, to note whether he is paying attention to you or is distracted by his surroundings. Once mounted, *begin* and *end* each ride with a few minutes of walking to loosen up before working and cool down before returning to the barn. Since horses are always encouraged to walk to and from the stable at the track, this mirrors the routine he knows best.

10.1 With time and careful preparation, the ex-racehorse can learn to travel rhythmically forward while maintaining a soft contact.

10.2 Riders at the track
commonly "bridge" the
reins, keeping a steady
pressure on the bit
while at the same time
stabilizing themselves in
the saddle.

Rein Tension Means "Go"

Racehorses are taught to "grab" the bit and run. The jockey or exercise rider "bridges" the reins (crosses them over the horse's withers and takes both reins in each hand, then presses down on either side of the withers or neck). Bridging keeps the horse "on the bit" and allows the rider to balance (fig. 10.2). It also allows the rider to maintain a steady hold on the reins and makes his position stronger: the horse pulls against himself rather than pulling the rider out of the tack.

I've mentioned before that although it is instinctive for many riders to take a tighter hold on the reins when slowing or stopping the horse, with an OTTB this can have the opposite, undesirable effect of making him want to go faster! Your longeing practice should have prepared the horse to submit to the bit, but it may take time for him to fully understand the different signals you are giving him from the saddle. Be patient and use your voice commands rather than relying solely on your reins, and learn to give and take the reins rather than just pull (see p. 185).

Keep Going Forward

When the horse is anxious, try to relax and focus on staying balanced rather than shortening the reins and tightening your grip. Keep the reins short enough to maintain control, but give the horse enough freedom of the head and neck so he does not feel restricted. Whether he bucks, rears, shies, or balks, always focus on *directing his energy forward*. Don't attempt to rein him in right away when he goes a little faster than you'd like—as long as he is going forward, he is doing what you asked him. You can slow him down, and work on balance and collection, after "forward" has been achieved.

Gradually Work toward Riding Alone

Do not be in a rush to ride the horse without a handler at your side. As he relaxes and becomes comfortable with you sitting on his back, you can gradually develop indepen-

dence from your helper on the ground. At New Vocations, we use a ground person until the horse is comfortable being mounted and remains calm at the walk—this may only take a couple of days, or it may take over a week. If you are retraining your first OTTB, plan to have someone nearby for several weeks, even after you no longer need him or her to hold your horse, as a safety precaution.

Getting Started Right

It is best to continue your horse's training under saddle in the same schooling area where he was longed, and later mounted and ridden for the first time. A solid rail or wall around the perimeter of the area helps keep the horse going straight ahead, and gives you more control. A big open field begs for trouble and gives your horse too much room to run if something spooks him.

For your early training under saddle, choose mild days with little to no wind, when the arena or paddock is quietest and without external distractions, just as you did when you started teaching your horse to longe. And, if your schedule allows, work your horse around same time each day with the same feed, turnout, and grooming schedule as you've already established. Always reserve plenty of time to groom your horse and tack up as it can be a relaxing preparation for ridden work.

10.3 Spend a few minutes longeing your horse in side reins prior to mounting. This encourages him to use his back and neck muscles properly.

comforting to have a person walk alongside them for a while. After a few rides you will learn what works best for your horse and you can tailor the warm-up routine to his needs and personality.

Seat, Legs, and Hands

Seat

Most exercise riders at the track weigh between 115 and 150 pounds. In the early stages, you should sit "lightly" on your horse's back as he gets used to carrying your weight—sitting tall and imagining yourself "light as a feather" can help. While it can work to have a smaller rider start your horse the first few times, the rider's ability to control his position in the saddle is more important than his actual weight.

Legs

Your legs should rest lightly on your horse's sides; if he overreacts to even slight leg pressure, put more weight in your stirrups to help keep your leg contact as minimal as possible (for more on leg pressure, see p. 164). As I said in chapter 9, each OTTB reacts differently to leg pressure; some are perfectly fine with it while others are extremely sensitive, especially at the beginning of the ride.

Hands

Your hands must be steady in order to main-

Before mounting, longe your horse for at least five to ten minutes to "get any bucks out" and loosen up his muscles and joints (see p. 120). For your first several rides, it is beneficial to include a couple of minutes in side reins, which will help the horse focus on working in a correct outline and encourage him to relax his neck and back muscles before you get on (fig. 10.3).

Get a leg-up or use a mounting block (see pp. 160 and 162), then allow your horse to just walk around, relax, and get used to his surroundings and your weight on his back. Some horses walk more calmly after trotting around a bit first. Insecure horses may find it

10.4 Racehorses often display a tendency to "hang" on the bit.

tain a light contact to the bit. Relax your elbows so they act like hinges, and allow your
arms—and thus your hands—to follow
the movement of the horse's head with an
"elastic" connection. If your elbow joints
are tense and locked, your hands will pull
against the horse's mouth. This, in turn,
causes *him* to tense up.

Many OTTBs like to "hang" on the bit
when being ridden. Exercise riders normally allow this as long as the horse is doing his
job (fig. 10.4). But, in his new life as a riding horse, he needs to learn that this is not
acceptable; he must learn to accept a light,
steady contact on his mouth while moving
forward. Longeing with side reins helps cor-

A

10.5 A & B When your OTTB gets heavy in your hands (A), encourage him to move forward on a slightly longer rein and lighter contact (B).

rect this prior to under saddle work (see p. 138), but some horses revert to hanging on the bit once a rider is on their back. You can teach your horse to trust the contact by maintaining the elastic connection from your hand to his mouth as explained on p. 177. Follow his motion and encourage him to move forward off your leg (figs. 10.5 A & B).

Do not fight with your horse if he also revisits old habits like head-tossing or over-flexing. The answer again is to remain giving with your hands and push him forward.

Rhythm and "Forward"

Focus on maintaining a consistent rhythm. The horse should be used to maintaining a rhythm at the canter from his days at the track, and your work on the longe line should have begun to establish steady rhythm at *any* gait. Once you are in the saddle, it is up to you to sense when he is slow or rushing. Do what you can to control your own body in order to have an effect on his—if he wants to rush at the trot, for example, "pulling" in response will only send an OTTB rushing forward even faster (see p. 174). Instead, use your body by

10.6 A & B Early in training, do not become overly concerned with your horse's head position. Even if he fiddles with the bit or throws his head, remain soft with your hands and focus on a steady, forward rhythm.

A

slowing your posting down (linger a little longer in the "up" phase), together with a light, steady contact on the reins.

This is not the time to be concerned with the horse's carriage or where his head position happens to be; working in a correct, rounded outline can come later. For now, you should simply send—or allow—the horse to go forward. As mentioned earlier, some horses will toss their head, pull against the bit, stick their head in the air, or tuck their chin in toward their chest to evade

the bit. Rather than pull against these evasions, send your horse steadily forward and "ride him through" the problem (figs. 10.6 A & B). If you do not focus on the bad behavior, and you do not allow him to dwell on it, but instead make him think about moving forward *always*, he will eventually realize it is more work to trot while tossing his head (for example), than it is to simply trot.

Halt and Half-Halt

A couple of important things for an OTTB to learn early in his training are the halt and half-halt. Racehorses rarely have to stand still for very long with a rider on their back, so at first, do not expect him to stand still for more than a second or two at the halt. The verbal command "Whoa" should have been confirmed on the longe line, giving you a place to build from under saddle.

Practicing the Halt

Your first transitions to halt should be from walk. Do not practice it from other gaits until your horse's walk-halts are accomplished calmly, without fuss.

How-To

1 Say, "Whoa," while sitting deep into the saddle with heels down and close your leg as you close your hands around the reins. Hold them still until the horse halts. If he doesn't halt after several strides, give and take on the reins until he does (see p. 185).

2 Once he stops, even if only for a second, immediately relax your seat, hands, and legs, and praise him.

3 Ask the horse to walk forward several steps before halting again.

This is a simple exercise, but it may take several days for the horse to understand. Gradually ask him to stand still a little longer, and eventually he will pay attention to your seat and hands, and stand quietly until you ask him to move forward again. Once you teach the horse that when you sit deep in the saddle you want him to slow down, you have taught him a key lesson that will help you ride him well in all three gaits.

Teaching the Half-Halt

A half-halt is an invaluable tool used for many purposes. It can help bring a horse's attention back to his rider, refocusing him and "waking him up." It can balance a horse in preparation for a transition, a turn, or any movement such as a circle or figure eight. It can also be used every few strides to rebalance or collect the horse. Whatever your discipline or riding goal, the half-halt is an important lesson.

The aids for the half-halt are closely related to the aids for halt: you ask by *closing your legs, sitting up tall,* and *closing your hands* all at the same time for only a couple seconds—then releasing the aids. A half-halt is a momentary action; as soon as it is performed, it is done. Concentrate on giving very clear aids in this exercise. OTTBs learn quickly and your horse will respond well to correctly given aids, but he will also get frustrated if you give him mixed signals (figs. 10.7 A & B).

As the horse starts to understand and respond to your half-halts, ask him to go forward while you maintain a steady contact with his mouth.

10.7 A & B The half-halt can be used as a corrective device when the horse loses concentration or fights the rider's hands (as shown in A), or to prepare the horse for a new movement. Close your legs and hands momentarily as if preparing for a full halt—the horse will respond by stepping underneath himself and coming back to your hand (A), and then move forward again refocused and better balanced (B).

Downward Transitions

Racehorses do not gallop flat out all the time—they are also trained to make *gradual* downward transitions to canter, then trot, and finally to walk at the end of a workout. In fact, riders are encouraged to never pull a horse to a complete stop from a gallop (or even a canter) unless the horse is injured. So, be prepared to allow your OTTB plenty of time to move from a faster to a slower gait when you first begin riding him.

Watch Your Body

Both pulling on the reins and lightening the seat are cues that to the OTTB mean "go forward," so if you A) pull back on the reins, and B) inadvertently bring your body forward out of the saddle when you do so, you might not get the reaction you are looking for! Instead, many horses respond by getting excited and rushing (figs. 10.8 A–C). You may have seen jockeys standing up in their stirrups at the end of a race as they slow their horse down, but this is to stretch their legs

10.8 A–C Pulling back (A) and leaning forward (B) mean "go" to the OTTB. If your horse is rushing at the trot, establish a slow, steady posting rhythm to slow him down without getting in a tug-of-war (C).

and at the same time give them leverage as they give and take on the reins. It is a practice appropriate for stopping a tired horse after a race, but it does not translate in the riding arena.

Give and Take

To get a calm, downward transition from your horse, ask by sitting down in the saddle, keeping your legs still and hands steady as you close them and yet allow them to follow the horse's motion. Use the verbal cues you taught him on the longe line along with continuous half-halts.

Remember, there is no point getting into a tug-of-war, since the thousand-pound horse underneath you will always win. If he does not listen and insists on going strongly forward, maintain steady contact with the outside rein while taking a firm contact on the inside rein (pulling back slightly) and then *releasing* it. Repeat this motion until the horse responds. (Note: he may turn slightly to the inside—allow him to do a large circle.)

As soon as he does, reward him by resuming the light, even contact.

If you pull steadily on the reins the horse will either increase his pace as I've mentioned before, or eventually become dull and stop paying attention. By "giving and taking" the reins instead, you ask him to stop or slow, give him a break by releasing, then remind him again of your request.

If your horse ever gets really out of control, and is ignoring your efforts to give and take the reins, turn him in a tight circle to get his attention and slow him down, or aim him at a barrier such as a fence or a wall. (Just make sure the fence is high enough so he stops, rather than jumping it!)

This exercise will encourage the horse to pay attention to your hands. When he is responsive to them, progress to doing circles and changes of direction (see below).

Bending and Turning

OTTBs tend to be stiff through their necks and backs, making it difficult for them to perform a turn—even a wide one—at the end of an arena. Remember, they are not used to making circles smaller than the size of a mile-long track! Work in the round pen and on the longe line introduces your horse to the idea of a smaller circle. To further encourage him to bend and supple his neck and back muscles, work on large circles, figure eights, and serpentines and make gradual changes of direction by crossing the diagonal.

The Rider's Hands

When circling, keep a steady contact on the *outside* rein near his withers. The rein should be long enough and the contact elastic to allow the horse to turn his head slightly to the inside. Use a slight opening rein with the *inside* hand, bringing your hand out toward your knee while keeping your elbow soft to guide the horse to the inside (fig. 10.9). To soften his jaw, give and take with your fingers on the inside rein, making sure to soften when the horse yields to you.

The Rider's Legs

Your *inside* leg should ask the horse to bend around it to prevent him from dropping his inside shoulder and rushing into the turn leaning in like a motorcycle, while your *outside* leg, positioned slightly behind the girth, steadies him and encourages him to go forward as he responds to your inside leg.

Every horse will react differently to the rider's leg. At the track riders use their legs for balance and rarely as an aid to move the horse's body laterally, so you should only start to introduce stronger leg aids when your horse is relaxed and balanced under you. Many OTTBs quickly learn how to appropriately respond to the leg; others may need more time to learn not to evade leg pressure by moving away more than is needed (see more on leg pressure on p. 164).

10.9 When circling or turning, keep your outside hand steady near the horse's withers while using an inviting "opening rein," bringing your inside hand back toward your inside knee.

Introducing Canter

For the first couple of weeks working your horse under saddle, just walk, trot, and halt during your training sessions. This allows you to develop a partnership with the horse and get him a little more "together" and relaxed at the slower gaits before you shift into the next gear and ask him to canter. Meanwhile continue to have him canter on the longe line, letting him figure out his balance without your weight on his back.

When your horse is responding to your halt, half-halt, and downward transition cues, and moves comfortably at the walk and trot, you can integrate cantering into his training regimen.

Using Two-Point

At the track, exercise riders ask for the canter by tightening their reins, taking the two-point position, squeezing with their legs, and clucking or making a kissing noise. The rider maintains this two-point position and holds the reins with a firm, steady hand while cantering.

Obviously, early in training you cannot expect your new horse to pick up the canter when you are sitting deep in the saddle, so to avoid confusing him start in a two-point position. Keep a steady, yet gentle hold on the reins and use the same verbal cue you use when asking him to canter on the longe line.

You may get more of a hand-gallop than a canter at first, but don't panic! It is best to just encourage the horse to go forward around the full arena or in a very large circle at whatever tempo he is most comfortable, even if it's a bit fast for your taste. In the beginning, just stay relaxed, don't pull back on the reins, and go with the flow; eventually as the horse becomes more comfortable and balanced, you can use half-halts to help regulate the horse's speed (see p. 182).

Some horses may benefit from the rider remaining in the two-point position in the early stages of training and being slowly introduced to the rider sitting (figs. 10.10 A & B). Others may be naturally comfortable with the rider sitting. This will encourage him to slow down, but be prepared for him to break into a trot. Because exercise riders sit down in the saddle and give and take on the reins when they want to transition to a trot on the track, most racehorses automatically trot when the rider sits at the canter—many will even tug against the reins as if to say, "I'm ready for you to 'give' me some rein now!" When this happens, allow the horse to relax and trot forward quietly rather than kicking him immediately back into canter. Always establish a steady, balanced trot before you ask for the canter again.

When you are ready to transition from the canter to the trot, sit up tall, sink your weight into the saddle, and close your hands on the reins, then release the aids when the horse responds (for more on downward transitions, see p. 184).

10.10 A & B Riders at the track ask for the canter in the two-point position. When first adding canter to your workouts, you can avoid confusing your OTTB by assuming this position rather than sitting down in the saddle during the transition.

On the Forehand

At the track, horses usually gallop slowly or canter on their forehand, *pulling* themselves along with their front legs rather than *pushing* with the hindquarters. Many will only drive from behind during a fast workout or during a race. Because of this, OTTBs may feel really "downhill" and unbalanced when you first canter. They need to develop strength in their hindquarters and back muscles before this can improve.

Longeing the horse with side reins helps him learn to balance himself, and when ridden, canter-to-trot transitions will improve the horse's strength, encourage him to pay attention to your aids, and create a more balanced, steady canter. Both exercises will improve the horse's ability to actually canter

The canter may invite the OTTB to revert to his "track ways," hanging on the bit and heavy on the forehand (A). However, he will eventually gain the muscle and balance necessary to perform a forward, uphill-feeling canter (B).

with power from behind, rather than gallop on the forehand. After several weeks of canter work under saddle, he should be strong, balanced, and responsive enough for you to push him forward into a closed hand to lift his head and front up (figs. 10.11 A & B).

Correct Canter Leads

As I discussed earlier (see p. 20), racehorses are taught to take the left lead in turns and the right lead on the straightaways preventing the horse's left side and left legs from taking all the strain of the gallop. Watch Thoroughbreds in a race and you may see many of them get their second wind by performing a flying change to the right lead as they enter the final stretch. Recognizing this practice, there are several key points to remember

when teaching your horse to take the correct lead in the arena:

1 Asking for the canter going into a corner helps the horse balance properly in order to pick up the correct lead.

2 Putting more weight in your outside stirrup frees up the horse's inside shoulder and hip.

3 Improving the canter in the direction of the lead your horse prefers before asking him to pick up the lead on his "weak" side allows the horse to become responsive to the aids in an "easy" direction. Then, when you tackle the lead he finds more difficult, he will at least understand on some level what you are asking him to do.

Flying Lead Changes

Note that horses learn to change their leads at speed when racing, so it's possible they will very suddenly change on their own in the arena. While you might eventually want to teach your OTTB flying lead changes, you will want them to be on command, and only after the basic gaits have been established. Pay close attention to your weight distribution in the saddle—jockeys encourage Thoroughbreds to switch leads on the turns and straightaways with a slight shift of weight and a rein aid. Your OTTB will be very sensitive to how you balance on his back.

When your horse *is* ready to incorporate flying lead changes into his canter work, the lesson should be an easy one to teach.

How-To

1 Begin by picking up the weak-side canter lead—for our purposes, let's say this is the right lead.

2 Canter several large laps to the right, then ask the horse to change rein across the diagonal.

3 Shift your weight into the right stirrup and pull your left rein slightly up and out toward the left, changing the direction of the horse's bend. Your right leg should stay just behind the girth, encouraging the horse to continue forward.

Most OTTBs will naturally switch from the weak to the strong canter lead with this simple exercise. You may find it more difficult going from the strong to the weak side. The addition of a ground pole on the diagonal can help instigate the change.

Lessons in Backing-Up

Most OTTBs are unfamiliar with the cue to back up or "rein-back." You should not attempt to teach your horse this important movement—a basic requirement in all disciplines—until he clearly understands leg, rein, and voice cues. The horse should be working well on the bit, and be supple and able to easily complete bending exercises at the walk, trot, and canter. He should not show any inclination to rear. When this is the case, then he is ready to back up.

Begin on the Ground

The best way to teach the rein-back is by starting on the ground. Your horse should be outfitted with a bridle for this exercise. I recommend practicing prior to each ride and again once you get off.

How-To

1 Stand on the left side of your horse, but in front of and facing his shoulder. Place your reins in your left hand and establish a light contact with the bit.

2 Give your horse the "go-forward cue" he

is familiar with (a cluck or kissing sound).

3 As he starts to go forward, pull gently back on the reins as if to stop him, but keep asking him to move—now backward—with your voice and increased contact with the reins. If your horse is confused and doesn't move backward, then take a step toward him and place your right hand on his shoulder, pushing slightly, to reinforce the back-up cue. In the early stages, one or two steps back is all you should ask for; then, immediately reward the horse, and ask for one or two more.

Never yank on the horse's mouth if he is not responding. At this point in his training, he should be willing to "give" his head to the rein pressure—you just need to encourage him to also move his body backward.

Once your OTTB understands *how* to back up, change your voice cue to "Back" instead of the go-forward verbal cue you used initially.

Training Rein-Back from the Saddle

Once the horse easily backs up on cue from the ground you can start asking him to do the same under saddle. At first it is very helpful to have a ground person on hand to assist when you ask for the rein-back.

How-To

1 Begin at the halt with a nice soft contact with the bit. Your ground person should stand on the left side of you, in front of and facing the horse's shoulder, as you did in preliminary rein-back lessons.

2 Gently squeeze your horse with both legs (the go-forward cue) while at the same time increasing the pressure on the reins and saying, "Back." Your helper should reinforce the cue by stepping forward toward the horse and placing one hand on his shoulder. Again, in the beginning one or two steps back is a great accomplishment and the horse should be rewarded. Release your rein and leg pressure and give him a pat.

Repeat this exercise several times then move on to a different lesson. Don't overdo it—at the most, work on the rein-back once or twice during a single riding session.

Identifying Riding Problems and Their Causes

Teaching your OTTB to walk, trot, canter, halt, and back up in the arena, as well as how to bend and flex, smoothly transition from gait to gait, and respond to half-halts is not a simple task to be taken lightly. It takes a great deal of patience to establish a strong, correct foundation under saddle, and you are bound to run into an array of bad habits and anxiety-based problems along the way.

The change in your horse's lifestyle and training program can throw him for a loop. Don't get frustrated; when you run into a problem, take a deep breath and fully evaluate the situation. You need to find the source of the issue in order to solve it and move on. Begin with a checklist of possible causes to identify and/or eliminate likely reasons for bad behavior.

Habit

Is the behavior a result of the work or management your horse experienced at the track? For example, when horses gallop they become used to leaning on the bit while the rider "bridges" the reins. This leaning "habit" is a problem in a riding horse. Bad habits may also be the result of nervous behavior, such as when a horse will not stand still for mounting. This may be due to anticipation of the workout ahead, and was likely never corrected at the track.

Pain

Is the horse experiencing, or perhaps anticipating pain? The horse may have developed aggressive or defensive behavior in response to discomfort. Pain may be dental, structural or skeletal (see p. 46), muscular (see p. 47), or due to poorly fitting equipment (see below).

Equipment

Does your equipment fit properly? The list of ways equipment can cause a horse to act badly is a long one. A few common culprits include:

- The bit—make sure it is the correct size with no rough edges, and adjusted appropriately (see p. 133).
- The saddle tree—it should be the correct width for the horse's back.
- The saddle pad—check that it is a suitable thickness for your horse's shape and the saddle's fit, and that it is free from burrs or dried sweat. Anything that pinches, rubs, or irritates the horse will obviously be reflected negatively.

I've recommended several books that can help you examine your equipment for fit and quality in the Resources, p. 246.

Environment

Are environmental distractions causing the horse to act out? Cars, dogs, lawn mowers, flapping tarps, and domestic animals that a racehorse may have never seen (like donkeys, pigs, or cows) can cause nervousness and bad behavior. Windy and cold weather also tends to make *all* horses more excited, especially when objects are blowing around.

Past Experience

Is the horse remembering something that happened in his past? Even when a horse had a good life at the track, there are going to be triggers that set him off. For example, if you eventually start to compete your horse, the loudspeaker may remind him of the call to the post, and the location of the show may resemble the track—or even be on or near one. These elements can inspire a relapse in anxiety-based behavior.

Separation Anxiety

Has your horse been turned out with others? Does he call to a friend or friends repeatedly and balk when leaving them? He may well have become a bit herdbound, and I've seen horses become nervous or anxious when asked to work apart from a "buddy."

Troubleshooting Three Common Problems

Here, I discuss three common issues people run into when retraining an ex-racehorse, the possible reasons for the behavior, and how one can go about working through it.

Nervous/Jigging

An anxious horse is often anticipating a track workout; it may take months for him to realize that he can just relax and is only going to walk at the beginning of a ride. If this is the case with your horse, focus on remaining calm with a light seat and steady hand. If you tense up and pull the reins tight, the horse will likely get more nervous—some may even bolt or rear. Restricting him will only frustrate him and encourage him to work against you.

Common Behavior Issues under Saddle

PROBLEM	POSSIBLE CAUSES
Head-Tossing	Poorly fitting bit or bridle; rider's rough hands; nervous habit; tooth problem; tongue over bit.
Open Mouth	Poorly fitting bit or bridle; nervous habit; tongue over bit; horse formerly ridden in drop, flash, or figure-eight noseband.
Tongue over Bit	Nervous habit; horse had his tongue tied; horse formerly ridden in a drop, flash, or figure-eight noseband; bit too low in mouth.
Bucking	Improperly fitting saddle or a badly fitting, rough, or worn saddle pad causing a sore back or withers; girth galls; biting insects and skin irritation; individual sensitivity (cold-backed); hind-end lameness; insufficient turnout leading to excess energy.
Rearing (often preceded by balking/refusal to move forward)	Poorly fitting bit; rider's rough hands; nervous habit; dislike of work; insufficient turnout leading to excess energy.

Put Him to Work

Remember that OTTBs are bred to be athletes, and so they always need a way to channel their energy. Plus, a nervous horse has *excess* energy to expend. Get your horse's at-

10.12 A & B When an OTTB insists on jigging nervously rather than walking (A), put his mind and body immediately to work by asking him to trot forward (B).

tention by putting him immediately to work (figs. 10.12 A & B). As long as the horse is not out of control, try to work *with* rather than *against* his energy by letting him go forward in a steady trot, and only ask for a walk again when he settles. Make big circles or figure eights to keep him thinking. (Note: avoid making small circles early in his training, because he still lacks the balance and strength to perform them safely.) This "put him to work" approach also helps to avoid "explosions."

Breathe

Rider tension transmits quickly to an OTTB, so try hard to keep your body relaxed and your breathing regular. You may feel a little silly, but taking a deep breath and then letting it out audibly will encourage your horse to do the same and help him relax. Work for five minutes or so, letting the horse move forward, and listen for him to sigh or snort; once a tense horse lets out his breath like this you know you're over the hump. Then ask for a transition down to the walk.

Early in training, one or two steps of walk are a big accomplishment for some horses. Reward him with a pat and allow him to move forward into trot again. Always remember, trying to force the horse to walk will probably just frustrate your horse and make him more difficult. Resist the urge to fight with him, and you'll succeed in calming him much sooner.

Rushing at the Trot

Many OTTBs simply do not know what speed is acceptable, so your goal is to help your horse think about his pace and listen to your aids. If your horse tends to rush at the trot, there are several ways to influence his speed.

Slow Your Rhythm

Slow your posting down rather than pulling on his mouth. (As I've explained, the latter is counterproductive—see p. 174.) Keep your hands soft with steady contact.

A

10.13 A & B At the
track, horses often evade
the bit by putting their
nose in the air, and
OTTBs will sometimes
revert to such habits
during retraining.

Downward Transitions

Ask for some trot-to-walk transitions, allowing the horse to trot several strides before asking him to walk. Walk for several steps and then ask for trot again. Performing downward transitions gets the horse's attention and helps regulate his pace.

Circles and Turns

Trot circles and changes of direction can also assist in slowing the horse down, since it is much easier to trot a circle at a slower speed than a fast one. As before, your hands must remain steady with a light contact, and your seat should maintain this slower tempo

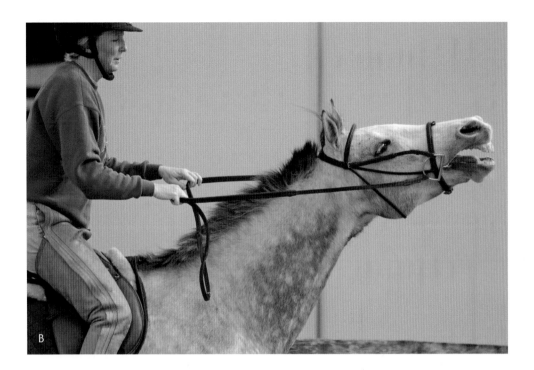

with deliberate, rhythmic posting as you ask the horse to bend or change direction.

Critique Yourself

Consider your riding and whether it could be the cause of your horse's rushing. When you are unable to maintain a stable seat you cannot set an even tempo for your horse to follow. If your seat is not yet independent (where you have individual control of its different elements) your aids will be inconsistent. In such cases, I recommend you have a more experienced and balanced rider work your horse in the early stages of his training.

Evading the Bit

Your horse may evade the bit either by sticking his nose in the air or by overflexing his poll and tucking his chin to his chest. When this happens, unless it is caused by dental problems, a poorly fitting bit, or the wrong bit, it is probably a trust-related issue or a habit developed during the horse's previous experience with a number of different riders on the track. Exercise riders don't usually mind when a horse hangs on the bit or evades it, as long as he keeps moving forward (fig. 10.13 A, and see further discussion, p. 177).

High-Headed

If your horse sticks his head and nose in the air as an evasion when you ride him (fig. 10.13 B), return to work on the longe

10.14 A & B Another common evasion is overflexion (A). Relax your elbows, and ride more with your seat and less with your hands while the horse learns to trust the rein contact (B). Note: in an effort to keep her hands soft, this rider has allowed her thumbs to turn in and her fingers to open a little more than is ideal.

line in side reins for a few weeks (see p. 138). The side reins provide a steady, dependable contact and the horse should begin to willingly move forward and relax and lower his head and neck as soon as he is confident he will not get hit in the mouth.

It may take several sessions of riding on a slightly loose rein or very light contact before you can slowly start to increase the contact. Keep your hands steady but elbows elastic to move with him as you ask the horse

to go forward. When he relaxes and yields to the pressure, reward him by softening—but maintaining—the contact and telling him he is "a good boy."

If the horse continues to evade the bit when you ride despite the work on the longe and riding with only light contact, do a self-check to make sure that *you* are maintaining a *steady* contact with his mouth. Unsteady hands constantly bump the bit and this often causes a horse to raise his

head in self-defense. A green OTTB is not the type of horse you should ride when you need to work on your own position.

Overflexion

If your horse evades the bit by overflexing his poll and carrying his head low and chin tucked, you are most likely too tense and rigid with your hands and arms, or too heavy-handed. *Relax* and *follow the motion* because he is trying to avoid unsteady bit pressure. Ride more with your seat and less with your hands.

Longeing with loose elastic side reins will help the horse understand that he can move forward and accept the bit without a hard or unsteady hand pulling on his mouth (see p. 146). Once he is able to stretch his neck and accept the bit on the longe, then the horse will be ready for a rider again—but the rider must have steady hands and consistent contact (figs. 10.14 A & B).

Ground Pole Exercise

In either case of bit evasion, trotting ground poles, spaced 4 to 5 feet apart, can help the horse to stretch his head and neck forward and down, and relax through his back. (For more information on working with ground poles, refer to chapter 11, p. 208.)

Making Training Fun

Just as it is important to establish a foundation for your OTTB's ridden training with groundwork, basic schooling under saddle is an important building block in his re-education. Before you can progress further, he should willingly go forward off your leg and have learned to accept your aids and the bit. Your focus should be keeping him relaxed and supple, and riding in a steady rhythm to help his mind and body develop correctly.

In the next chapter, I discuss riding your horse outside the arena. This is a big step and should only be taken once you and the horse are completely comfortable working together in the usual, enclosed environment. If you are just starting out with your OTTB, this may seem like a distant reality—it doesn't have to be. Let me remind you of several ways to ensure your training plan progresses successfully and in a timely manner.

Quality, Not Quantity

Keep in mind that workouts at the track are relatively short. When starting an OTTB's training as a riding horse, 15 or 20 minutes work overall should be sufficient; he will not be ready for a 45-minute or hour-long training session until later in his career. Like young children, OTTBs have limited attention spans, so aim for a short, positive lesson. With training, your horse will mature and become stronger and you can gradually increase the length of his training sessions.

Consistency

OTTBs leave the track with lots of ability, both mental and physical, but lack the training to understand many "basic" riding skills. Unfortunately, because Thoroughbreds are smart and eager to please, they get easily frustrated by confusing or conflicting signals. The more consistent you are with your aids, praise, and corrective action, the quicker your horse will learn what you want.

Small, Easily Completed Tasks

Your objectives for the horse's training should be simple: as I said, OTTBs typically aim to please and have a good work ethic, but they don't like to be confused. If you sense that your horse is getting upset, slow down, and focus on small tasks he can easily complete—for instance, halt-walk or walk-trot transitions, giving him plenty of time to make each one. At first, you may have to let the horse take as many as 15 trot steps before he walks, but patiently focus on eventually making it ten, then five, then two.

End on a Good Note

Keep the experience positive by finishing each training session with something that the horse understands and can perform eas-ily, even if it is just trotting a large circle. In addition, if the horse is relaxed and calm at the end of a workout, finish with a long walk on a loose rein. This is a good way for him to wind down after concentrated hard work. It will let him relax and learn to enjoy being ridden without any pressure to perform—and it has the added benefit of helping him cool down after his workout.

11

Phase Five: Moving toward a New Vocation

So far, your horse's training has been focused on giving him a foundation of basic skills. As with the construction of a house, your horse's primary training needs to be solid—without missing elements as the result of cutting corners along the way. If you begin building on it and adding new lessons before it is complete, you run the risk of overwhelming your horse physically and/or mentally.

By this point you should have developed a strong, trusting relationship with your OTTB. He is working comfortably in all three gaits in the arena and has a good understanding of voice, hand, seat, and leg aids—both forward and sideways. You are now ready to build on this foundation with the lessons in this chapter:

1 Introducing your horse to new objects and situations
2 Beginning exercises over ground poles
3 Going on your first trail ride
4 Taking your horse to his first clinic or schooling show

New Sights and Sounds

In today's hectic world, horses need to be able to tolerate just about anything: kids on bicycles, barking dogs, golf carts whizzing around, motorbikes, low-flying airplanes, and who knows what else! Trails often cross or border busy roads and highways, and barns in many areas are surrounded by other homes and buildings, along with the hustle-and-bustle that goes with them. In any kind of competitive scenario, the modern world of sponsorship means that there will be lots of brightly colored banners and flags flapping around arenas and warm-up areas. Sound systems and large digital monitors are becoming standard. Show jumps get brighter and more outrageous in size, shape, and décor each year; even cross-country jumps aren't looking so "natural" these days, with oversized wood-carved animals and super-technical combinations showing up on courses. With all of these potential threats to your horse's sanity looming in your future, I suggest you expand your horse's horizons by introducing him to a variety of new situations now!

Whether you intend to turn your OTTB into a quiet trail horse or a brave eventer, it is best to first introduce weird and scary objects within the safe confines of the riding arena where he is now accustomed to working. Here you are in a controlled, enclosed area that has figured into his routine for some time: the footing is consistent, the fence provides a barrier, and the activity around the arena probably does not vary too much. The more your horse is exposed to in this "comfort zone," the more prepared he

11.1 Providing your OTTB a firm educational foundation through consistent work on the ground and under saddle will allow you to build new skills in a progressive manner, eventually culminating in a happy, healthy pleasure or competitive mount.

will be when faced with new challenges out in the open. Plus, it gives you an opportunity to learn how he responds to new sights and sounds, and therefore be ready to handle them in the future.

Training Methods

There is plenty that you can introduce to your horse in the confines of the arena to "desensitize" him: ground poles, cavalletti, jumps, barrels, traffic cones, tarps, even lawn chairs. To introduce him to a new object, you can:

- Approach it gradually, allowing him to see, smell, and touch it (you can start on the ground or in the saddle).
- Longe him in the arena with the object placed nearby.
- School alongside a "lead" horse—preferably a quiet, tractable mount—ridden by a friend to show your horse that the object is not a big deal.

Let's pretend that your horse spooks at the lawn chair every time he walks past your front yard. Do not immediately force him to confront the very scary chair. Instead, ride or lead him past it at the walk from a safe distance, patting him and praising him after he goes by (figs. 11.2 A & B). Do this a few times, and each time, walk a little closer to the chair, until before he knows it, he walks directly up to it. By keeping his attention focused on you, the chair will not be such a big deal.

Longeing with the lawn chair nearby works in a similar manner. If you keep your horse busy, asking him to focus on his lesson, it will be difficult for him to find the time to spook or shy. If you work him for several days with the chair in the ring, it will eventually become part of the environment and no longer be considered a threat.

Finally, a brave, calm experienced horse that has "seen it all" can be a great influence on a green horse. Since horses tend to feed off each other's reactions, the older horse acts as a good role model. Ride by the chair with another rider on just such a horse, and you'll find your OTTB less inclined to make a fuss over it.

You may not realize it, but you can have the same effect on your horse as the brave equine role model. If you are calm and relaxed then your horse will sense it and grow more confident. When you tense up and get nervous your horse will probably do the same.

When introducing new experiences, never get angry or upset or try to force your horse to face something he is not ready for. If you discipline a sensitive Thoroughbred with a strong hand you will only instill more fear. OTTBs respond positively when they have a patient handler who is willing to take the time to help them overcome their fears, whatever they are.

11.2 A & B First introduce your horse to strange objects, such as cones and lawn chairs, in an enclosed arena. Walk him past the object(s) at incrementally shorter distances, always praising him for a job well done.

Making It Part of the Lesson Plan

Plan training time to address new or strange sights and sounds. Schedule sessions specifically focused on desensitizing your horse, or casually add objects to your work area to incorporate into your regular daily lesson. I recommend working with:

- Cavalletti
- Ground poles
- Lawn chairs
- Umbrellas
- Potted plants
- Tarps
- Traffic cones
- Wheelbarrows
- Trash cans

Look around the barn and you are sure to find a few things that, when out of their usual element, could be considered "spookworthy." Air out your blankets on the rails of the riding arena; have a helper spray out your feed and water buckets alongside the ring while you're schooling; ask a friend to play various ringtones on your mobile phone at full volume as you ride by—be creative!

The Benefits of Ground Poles

Ground poles are a useful training tool for any intended discipline, as well as essential for teaching a horse to jump. They offer myriad benefits, and can often help troubleshoot problems before they get out of hand.

Awareness of Feet and Ground

Ground poles help your horse focus on where he is putting his feet, which is just as important for a trail horse or dressage prospect as it is for an eventer or a jumper. OTTBs often have a hard time paying attention to where they are putting their feet because they are so distracted by their surroundings. It is not uncommon for a horse to either spook at or trip over the first ground pole he is presented with, but continued ground pole training will encourage the horse to become aware of his feet and where they are going.

Correct Muscles and Self-Carriage

When you ask your horse to step over several poles in a row, he has to engage the muscles in his neck, back, and hindquarters to do so successfully. Many OTTBs have a tendency to trot around with a hollow back, stiffening against the hand and resisting the rider's aids. However, it is hard to trot over a series of poles with a stiff, hollow back, so the horse will naturally be encouraged to use and develop correct musculature.

Rhythm and Adjustability of Stride

Spacing ground poles encourages the horse to maintain a rhythmic gait. Varying the spacing teaches him to compress and elevate his stride, or lengthen it.

Straightness

You can use ground pole "guides" to "channel" your horse into a line (first, of ground poles, and later cavalletti or cross-rails). This helps him develop a straight approach to obstacles.

Courage

Consistent work over ground poles can inspire courage. Most OTTBs are somewhat apprehensive early in their training, but ground poles are a safe and straightforward way for a horse to learn a new lesson that will likely have a positive outcome. The positive experience will also teach him to trust you, which will help him be brave whenever he is faced with new obstacles.

Foundation for Jumping

Ground poles are invaluable when preparing the horse to jump. Without ever jumping a fence the horse develops a steady rhythm and consistent length of stride, stays in a straight line as he navigates an obstacle, and learns how to maneuver his body, becoming even more careful with his feet as he strives to trot or canter over the poles without touching them. Once your horse comfortably walks, trots, and canters over a series of ground poles then he's ready for the addition of cavalletti—poles raised off the ground— or small cross-rails. Many people want to rush into jumping without establishing a foundation over ground poles, but taking the time to master this basic step will build your horse's confidence and technique. Later, this will help discourage him from rushing, stopping, or running out as the jumps get higher.

Getting Started with Ground Poles

You can introduce the horse to ground poles under saddle or on the longe line. At this point, some horses may be brave and balanced enough, and their riders secure enough, to approach a ground pole (or poles) under saddle. At New Vocations, I generally prefer to longe horses over them first. Not only is it safer for the rider, enabling him to gauge the horse's reaction from a distance, but it also eliminates "interference" from the rider's hands and legs, giving the horse freedom to use his body as he learns to navigate the poles.

As applies to every phase of a young horse's training, the introduction to ground poles requires patience from the handler and rider. Though it takes more time to go step-by-step—never rushing or pushing the horse—your patience will pay off with a calm, confident and better-educated horse. If you rush him you will build a weak foundation that cracks under the pressure as training becomes more complex.

Longeing

Prepare the ring ahead of time for your first lesson. The poles can be "lying around" as you warm up to allow the horse to get used to them. I find it helpful to have a ground person on hand to set up the poles when the horse is ready to work.

I recommend a "heavy" cotton longe line for longeing your horse over ground poles. I find the thin, nylon styles are too lightweight and tend to flap around. (See p. 120 for more about outfitting the horse for longe work.)

You should warm up the horse with his usual routine before you start schooling the ground poles. Five or ten minutes should be sufficient.

He should be relaxed, but not overtired. If he is excited he will be less receptive to your commands; if your horse has already worked hard, it might be overwhelming to introduce something new—call it a day and wait until the next lesson.

Starting with a Single Pole

Have your ground person place a single ground pole on the longe circle. Shorten the line and lead the horse over to the pole (fig. 11.3). Allow him to look at it and sniff it, then ask him to step over. Each horse reacts differently to seeing poles on the ground. Some of them step right over a single pole without a second thought, while others will spook at the pole and not want to go near it

11.4 Longeing the horse over a single ground pole will help him gain confidence as he begins to accept it as part of his work environment.

(see my advice on p. 206 if you have trouble). Walk over the pole in one direction, then turn around and walk back over it. Once he is willing to walk over it in both directions with you accompanying him, put him back on the longe circle and let him walk, and then trot over it by himself (fig. 11.4).

Adding Poles

Once your horse is happily longeing over a single ground pole at the walk and trot, add more poles, spacing them about 4 to 5 feet apart, depending on your horse's length of stride. They should be evenly spaced on a straight line—you may have to move with

Adding Canter

Only ask your horse to canter over ground poles once he is confident and relaxed trotting over them. Canter poles should be introduced in the same way, beginning with a single pole. Start by trotting the horse over the pole several times until he is relaxed, then ask him to canter over it.

The horse's first reaction may be to jump the pole; be sure to move with him if he does. Practice going over the single ground pole until the horse does so quietly, then add additional poles. Canter poles should be spaced 9 to 12 feet apart depending on the length of the horse's stride, but in the beginning, I like to space the poles an extra stride apart, say 18 to 24 feet (curving with the longe circle), to give the horse more room to figure the exercise out.

Under Saddle

I recommend longeing your OTTB over ground poles until he is obediently walking, trotting, and cantering over them—and only then adding a rider. As I mentioned in the last chapter, with OTTBs, it is important to have a secure seat and be able to follow the horse's motion no matter what he is doing underneath you. An inexperienced horse may jump over the poles or take erratic steps when he is starting out, and an insecure rider may find it difficult to maintain a balanced position. Sitting heavily on the horse's back or hanging on his mouth accidentally will

your horse and alter the shape of the longe circle to accommodate them.

I have found that some horses try to jump over two poles, thinking a ditch lies between them, so moving from one to three poles is often the better transition (a horse is less likely to try to jump three poles at once). Adjust the poles if the distance between them seems uncomfortable for your horse, and add or take away poles to make the exercise more or less difficult (figs. 11.5 A & B).

11.5 A & B Once the horse is comfortable walking and trotting over a single pole, add poles, adjusting the distance between them to accommodate his stride.

make him apprehensive about the poles and cause difficulty at the next lesson.

If you feel prepared and confident in your horse's ability to approach ground poles with you in the saddle, then proceed with this lesson. It is helpful to have a ground person on hand to move the poles and adjust them as necessary.

Your Seat and Reins

As the rider, you should assume the half-seat (two-point position) in the early stages of ground pole work. This seat encourages your horse to lift and use his back. Your horse should readily understand lateral leg pressure at this stage of training, so you can encourage him to go directly over the center of the poles with your legs. Add guide poles if necessary (see p. 216).

Maintain a light, steady contact, allowing the horse to stretch his head and neck forward and down as he navigates the poles. Allow him to figure out the exercise without interference from your hands: holding the reins tightly or grabbing the horse's mouth when he takes a bad step only makes him nervous and insecure about the new experience. Grab mane if necessary to keep yourself steady and *never* yank him in the mouth.

Introducing the Poles

Begin, as usual, with a light warm-up before approaching the first pole. Then introduce one ground pole at the walk, allowing the horse to stop and sniff it at first, if he likes, but encouraging him to walk forward over it without hesitation (figs. 11.6 A & B). You don't want him to get in the bad habit of stopping in front of anything—poles or jumps—later on. It may be easier to have your ground person lead the horse forward the first time you ride him over a pole. Remember to reward the horse by making a big deal out of him with a pat on the neck and verbal encouragement when he does well.

When he is comfortable with one pole, add one or two more at the walk. Once this is handled easily, ask him to trot over a single pole. Your horse should willingly trot directly over the center of the pole without hesitation before you move on, adding two more poles (figs. 11.7 A & B). It sometimes helps to walk over the new series, first, then follow at a trot. Remain alert and ready for anything, but keep your seat and hands soft and relaxed so that you can follow the horse's movement without interfering with him. If he jumps or steps awkwardly, keep your leg on, your seat and hands steady, and just send him forward. Repeat the exercise until he understands and does it correctly.

As with using ground poles on the longe line, you should not ride your horse over poles at the canter until he is happily managing them in a workmanlike manner at the trot. Introduce a single ground pole first, and proceed as with the other gaits (figs. 11.8 A & B, and see more on cantering ground poles on p. 192).

11.6 A & B Under saddle, begin again with one pole at the walk; when the horse is comfortable and willing, add poles to create a series.

11.7 A & B Next, trot over a single ground pole, and then a series, concentrating on traversing the middle of the poles and keeping a steady rhythm.

Guide Poles

If your horse is "crooked" and has a hard time going over the center of the poles, or if he tries ducking out and going around the poles, a *guide pole* (or two) can be used to keep him straight. Place a single pole alongside the track at a 90 degree angle with the first ground pole, and in the corner formed by the poles, prop one end up. The visual line formed will help guide the horse directly over the poles. Doing this along the fence line, or adding a second at the other end of the first ground pole forms a "channel" to send the horse straight over the obstacle.

Guide poles can be used to keep the horse straight at the walk, trot, or canter.

Circle Size and Direction

During the early stages of work with ground poles keep the horse on a large circle (when longeing, you may have to adjust your circle to accommodate the poles), which gives him just enough time to regroup between poles without losing focus. Generally, the poles should be arranged in a straight line, not curved, so the distance between them does not vary from inside to outside. Reserve that lesson for later training (see p. 217).

11.8 A & B Cantering over ground poles is taught in the same manner, beginning with a single pole and adding another when your horse is comfortable with the exercise.

Work in both directions to avoid the horse becoming one-sided. You may find that, initially, he may be surprised to see the poles when he changes direction. If this happens, back up a step and reintroduce them by reducing speed or the number of poles until he goes over them calmly.

Two Extension/Collection Exercises

Strive to vary the lesson and keep it fresh and fun for your horse. OTTBs tend to have a short attention span and creative exercises will help to focus him and keep him looking for what comes next. Here are a couple of exercises I like to use once the horse is comfortable working over ground poles at all three gaits.

Lesson 1

Longe or ride the horse at the trot over sets of three or four poles arranged on a circle with the ends on the "inside" of the circle closer together and the ends on the "outside" further apart. The space between the poles should still measure 4 to 5 feet from the middle of one pole to the middle of the next. By sending the horse out on a larger circle, the poles will lengthen his stride, while bringing him in on a smaller circle will encourage him to take shorter steps. Extending a gait engages different muscles in the horse's body than compressing a gait does, so mix it up. This also prevents the horse from getting bored.

Lesson 2

In a large work area, place two different sets

11.9 It is best to have a bombproof "buddy" along when introducing the OTTB to new work areas or environments.

Out and About: Leaving the Arena

Trail riding or hacking out is good exercise and a great way to expose your horse to new sights and sounds. But, setting off into the woods before your horse is ready could leave a lasting negative impression that will take time to overcome. Even though OTTBs have seen a lot at the track, up to this point, their experience under saddle both at the track and at home has been in a controlled environment. Beyond the rail of the arena, anything can—and will—happen, and your horse needs to be prepared to handle the unexpected.

The key to preparing your horse to calmly go on a trail ride is to break it down into small steps.

The "Buddy System"

When you first take your horse outside his familiar work place, ask a competent rider on a steady, experienced horse to accompany you, if possible. Everything is easier for a green horse when he has a buddy, and as you know, OTTBs are used to having a lead horse with them at the track, so the routine will be comfortable and familiar. Your horse may need to go out in company for several weeks, and while some horses are eventually confident to ride out alone, others will always be happiest with a buddy along for the ride (fig. 11.9).

of four or five poles at different locations. Set one group of poles with 4 feet between each and the second group with 5 feet. Ride your horse at the trot over both groups in varied patterns, changing direction and adding circles to keep it interesting. The differing space between poles will make your horse think, encouraging him to lengthen or shorten his stride according to the pole placement.

Remember, the "buddy" horse needs to be really bombproof, since horses tend to feed off each others' reactions.

Step 1: Cool Down Outside the Arena
To begin, take a short walk around the outside of the arena or back to the barn following a successful schooling session (fig.11.10). This will expand the horse's boundaries without removing him from an area that is already familiar. If he is comfortable with this baby step, he is likely ready for a bigger step. If not, arrange for another horse and rider (a quiet, experienced pair—see p. 218) to accompany you a few times to boost his confidence before you move on.

Step 2: Ride in a Large, Enclosed Field
When your horse is comfortable in familiar territory, expand his horizons by working him in a large, enclosed pasture. The fence is an important element because it will offer your horse some security in this new, open space, and once under saddle it may prove useful for getting him under control if he gets overly excited.

For your first ride out in the larger field, choose a day with temperate weather—you are just asking for trouble if you try this step on a cold, windy day! Warm weather, on the other hand, could work to your advantage since the horse is more likely to feel relaxed and a little tired in the heat.

Ride the horse in the arena first to warm him up in a familiar environment and to

11.10 Introduce the OTTB to being ridden outside the arena by walking him back to the barn after a workout.

make sure his attention is focused on you. Then, walk him to the pasture (preferably with a buddy). If he his nervous he may benefit from a brief time on the longe line in the open pasture (figs. 11.11 A & B). This allows

11.11 A & B When working for the first time in an enclosed field, longe your horse in a corner formed by the fence line prior to mounting.

him to take in his surroundings and relax before you get back on. Choose a level corner of the pasture so that he has two sides of fencing to support him.

Once he is calm on the longe line, mount and proceed with your lesson. As always, take it one step at a time. Too many new experiences in one day will overwhelm him and set his training back. For some horses, one circuit of the field at a walk is enough for the first ride; next time try for two laps, and add a couple of circles and other school figures.

Each time out, if your horse feels ready, you can ask for a little bit more. The main goal is to keep him calm and relaxed; if he gets excited, work with him until he comes back to a quieter frame of mind. If he gets too worked up out in the open, take him back to the arena and work for a little while until the tension goes away and you can end the lesson on a positive note.

I recommend riding the horse in the fenced-in field on a regular basis, gradually progressing to all three gaits, and practicing

11.12 Ride your horse around the stable yard, down driveways, and in other unfamiliar areas near "home" to allow him to adjust to new sights, sounds, and terrain.

lots of transitions to make sure that he pays attention to you. Circles and figure eights also keep him focused and in control.

Step 3: Explore the Farm or Stable Area

When your horse is consistent and confident in the field, ride him through other paddocks and fields, over uneven ground, around the house, barns, sheds, trees, shrubbery, and automobiles. Take him out the day after it rains and, if you know that the footing is sound, walk him through puddles to get

him used to water. Expose him to as much as possible within the immediate area (fig. 11.12).

Step 4: Hit the Trail

When you feel that your horse is ready to head out on his first trail ride away from the ring, field, and barnyard, follow the same guidelines as earlier: wait for peaceful weather and bring a bombproof buddy (figs. 11.13 A & B) In addition, since OTTBs are usually thin-skinned and tend to be extremely sensi-

11.13 A & B Bring a buddy along the first few times you take your OTTB on the trail, and don't be surprised if your horse is a bit "looky" or nervous. Remain calm and rely on the quiet companion horse to reassure your mount.

tive to insects, it is a good idea to go out only when pests are unlikely to be bothersome. Though fly spray certainly helps, its potency only lasts a short time and one persistent deerfly can soon turn your horse's first trail ride into a disaster.

Plan the ride thoroughly beforehand. For the first outing, 20 to 30 minutes on the trail should be plenty. Know exactly where you will go and make note of which areas are likely to make the horse apprehensive: streams, downed trees, deer, leaves blowing or falling can all cause the horse to become nervous. Think through each possible trou-

ble spot and how you will approach it (fig. 11.14). By this time you and your horse should have a trusting relationship, so with reassurance from you and the added confidence from a lead horse, he should be able to mentally work through most of the obstacles you will face.

Most OTTBs tend to be nervous on their first few trail rides or short hacks, and some may continue to be apprehensive for the first year or more. However, once they get used to the "great outdoors," most come to enjoy the break from their usual training sessions and find the time out of the ring

11.14 Here, an OTTB
learns to calmly cross
a water obstacle. Try
to anticipate possible
trouble spots before
heading out for a trail
ride, and form a plan of
action before reaching
challenging points
on the trail.

therapeutic. Trail riding works wonders on a horse's mind, body, and soul in the same way that it helps overworked and stressed people unwind. If your horse has started to sour due to all the training in the ring; if he works in the arena for 15 minutes and then starts balking or pinning his ears as if to say, "I'm done!" then unstructured riding like hacking-out can help him learn to enjoy being ridden again.

Away from Home

Many OTTBs go on to have successful careers as show horses in a variety of disciplines (see p. 229). However, before you take your horse to his first training clinic or show, there is much more to teach him than we can cover in this book. That said, there are some foundational steps that will help the horse mentally prepare for the experience.

Work in the Arena with Other Horses

I have at various times throughout this book recommended that you employ a "buddy" horse to serve as a role model for your OTTB, so your horse may be somewhat accustomed to working in the ring alongside one other horse. Now it is time to increase the group size in preparation for lessons, clinics, and competition. First, work your horse while two others are being ridden, then three (depending on the size of your arena). At first, I recommend longeing your horse while the larger group works nearby. On the longe line the horse can gradually get used to the commotion and you can get a feel for how he will act in a crowded situation.

"Test Runs"

Before taking the horse into a busy or possibly chaotic environment where both of you are experiencing the pressure of performance, it is a good idea to have a test run or two in order to feel out your horse's reaction to trailering to a strange place. Some OTTBs will associate travel with racing and automatically become anxious. Others, finding themselves in a new place with unfamiliar horses, will become nerved up in anticipation for what they expect to come. Therefore, arrange your first outing(s) to be at a friend's farm or a local training facility where you can school him quietly and without any expectations.

Take the opportunity to establish a travel/arrival routine, including leg wrapping and unwrapping, loading and unloading, hand-walking, tacking-up, longeing, and so on. A familiar routine will help calm your horse when you begin to take him into other, more intense scenarios. Make mental note of what seems to upset your horse and what helps him relax. This knowledge will help you better prepare your horse for his next trip.

When you arrive at your "trial" destination, if possible, allow the horse to relax in a stall and take in the new place for a little while. If he seems upset, give him plenty of time to settle down. Then, take him out and lead him around the grounds. (Don't forget to put the chain over his nose!) If he seems fairly calm, find a *quiet* corner and work him lightly on the longe line. Do not try to longe him in a crowded arena or warm-up area, as it will increase the likelihood of an accident injuring you, or others. If all goes well, call it a day and return home.

Plan another test run, stay a little longer, and school him under saddle. Then on your next trip, increase the difficulty of the training session or add other horses and riders to the equation. The more short outings like this, the better; the more your horse is exposed to, the more comfortable he will be when it is time for him to eventually enter the show ring.

Clinics

When you take your horse to his first clinic, it is best to plan to arrive the day before it starts to give your horse plenty of time to settle in. Be sure to stick closely to your horse's usual travel routine and general timetable, including feed, mucking-out, and turnout (if a paddock is available).

Once your horse has adjusted to his stall and had a walk around the grounds, longe him in the arena where the clinic is to be held, giving him a chance to get used to the space and introduce him to anything spooky in the vicinity, like a viewing area or tent. If he is quiet, a short workout in side reins will help him focus. If your horse is too overly excited to longe calmly, hand-walk him and give him the day to adjust.

On the day of the clinic, I recommend planning a short longeing session to reacquaint your horse with the workspace and get any extra energy or bucks out. After he warms up, add the side reins to encourage him to concentrate on his job. Do not overwork him—just do enough so that you and he are prepared by the clinic's start time.

If the clinic begins and at any point you find it is too much for your horse to handle, quietly explain the situation to the clinician and your fellow riders, ask your horse to do something you know he can do easily, and exit the ring on a positive note. By reading your horse and leaving before he becomes out-of-control, you not only avoid his always associating clinic-type scenarios with fear or anxiousness, you also prevent a dangerous situation from developing. The clinician will respect your decision and think you the better horse person, and in the end, your horse will benefit.

Shows

Plan to attend your OTTB's first horse show or competition without actually competing. Go to this event with an open mind—allow your horse to take in the sights and sounds and tell you what he is, or is not ready to do. Some horses just need to hang out and do very little, while others may be ready to be ridden around the show grounds.

As with the first clinic, try to arrange to stable the horse overnight on the competition grounds. Give him plenty of time to settle in his stall before taking him out on short little strolls around the area. As discussed earlier, pay close attention to his body language and notice what makes him comfortable or uncomfortable. If he seems overreactive, longeing in a quiet spot can help him burn off extra energy before hand-walking (fig. 11.15).

At hunter, schooling, or local shows the competition rings are often open for schooling on the day before the show. This is a good time to introduce your horse to the arena without many other horses and people to distract him. The loudspeaker, which sometimes reminds OTTBs of the call to the post, is probably turned off at this time, as well.

11.15 Remember, OTTBs thrive on routine, so at a show, use the same techniques as you use at home to help your horse relax. Here, longeing in side reins in a quiet corner settles the OTTB and prepares him for work.

If the show ring itself is not open, there are always official warm-up areas that can serve a similar purpose. Progress in a similar manner as you would when preparing for a clinic: walk your horse around the ring, longe him without and with side reins, and if he takes it all in stride, lightly school him under saddle. This should not be a demanding workout, but simply an exercise in learning to perform in a strange environment.

If all goes well, your horse may be mentally ready to compete at the next show;

Two Common Obstacles at a Horse Show

The PA System

Announcements made over a PA (public-address) system often bring back memories of the announcer at the racetrack. Taking your OTTB to several shows without asking him to compete will help him get used to the various sounds, as well as the volume, often related to such a system. Your horse will soon realize that he is not going to be asked to race every time he hears this particular noise.

Congested Warm-Up Areas

Horse show warm-up areas are notoriously congested and chaotic spaces as many riders try to school their horses, and trainers try to school their riders, often while paying little attention to each other. It is unlikely that your OTTB will be recognized as a green horse, so be prepared to be crowded, cut off, and otherwise given inadequate space. It may help to tie a red ribbon in your horse's tail—this widely recognized symbol is generally used to indicate a horse kicks, but I find it is a better-

heeded warning than a green ribbon (often used on a green horse), which isn't as well known.

Another problem for the OTTB in close quarters is when a horse passes him—he may become anxious and speedy (racing habits die hard!), even when at the trot. This is one good reason for schooling your horse in company before bringing him to such a setting (see p. 224). Be sure your downward transitions and "Whoa" are well confirmed, too.

Taking an inexperienced, hot horse into a crowded warm-up area puts yourself and others at risk. If you are unsure of your horse's ability to handle the situation, find a less busy spot or wait until there is less activity in the warm-up area before you ride. And, before entering the fray, make sure that all of the other horses are in control so you are not adding to an already unstable scenario.

Note that at many shows, longeing is not allowed in warm-up areas; check with show management to see if there is a quiet corner designated for these purposes.

however, remember that the goal is to have a positive learning experience, not bring home ribbons. If the horse is asked to do too much too soon, the experience can have negative consequences. Some horses need to attend several competitions as "spectators" before they relax, while others may only need one trial run before they are ready to participate. Read your horse, learn to anticipate his reactions, and alter your plans accordingly.

12 Becoming a Success Story

Closing Thoughts

In this book I have covered the steps to developing a basic riding educational foundation for your OTTB. This means that, for you and your horse, the journey has only just begun.

It is my hope that in following my guidelines you have successfully reconditioned your horse, mentally and physically, eliminating health issues and stress-induced anxieties along the way. This, along with a skill set that includes proper ground manners, walking, trotting, cantering, and halting on the longe line and under saddle, means that your OTTB is now ready to move on and focus on the individual requirements of his new career. I strongly suggest finding a trainer to help you and your horse with this next step and eventually excelling in the mounted discipline of your choosing.

In this final chapter, I offer a glimpse of what some people have been able to accomplish with their OTTBs. A few of these stories are about professionals who trained their ex-racehorses to the highest levels of their sport, but the majority are about ordinary people—caring horse lovers who wanted to give a Thoroughbred a new chance at life. I hope that these profiles will inspire you to continue helping your horse become a success story, too.

There are many things for you and your horse to enjoy in your future together. I wish you the best on your journey—and I thank you for giving an OTTB the opportunity to pursue a new vocation.

Keen
(Money Broker-Mabel Victory)

Owner/Rider: Hilda Gurney
Discipline: Dressage

Achievements

Perhaps the most famous OTTB success story is that of Keen and Hilda Gurney. In a sport dominated by Warmbloods, Keen (1966–1989) stands out as a truly exceptional example of the Thoroughbred breed. A 17.2-hand gelding trained by California dressage pioneer Hilda Gurney, Keen reigned in the US dressage scene in the mid-1970s. A true ambassador for a sport that was just developing in the US at the time, he earned five USDF FEI-level Horse of the Year titles in 1974, 1976, 1977, 1978, and 1979. In addition, he and Gurney won team gold and individual silver medals at the 1975 Pan American Games in Mexico City, and at the Montreal Olympic Games in 1976—an historic moment in the history of American dressage—the pair placed fourth individually and helped bring home the team bronze, the first US Olympic medal in dressage since 1948.

12.1 Providing your OTTB a thorough re-education as outlined in this book will give him the basic skills necessary to begin a new career, like Key Slew, who now competes at Training Level events with his rider, Abby Leathers.

Keen went on to place fourth in the Grand Prix Special in Aachen, Germany, and seventh at the World Championships at Goodwood, England, in 1978. The following year Keen was largely undefeated in the US, and at the Pan American Games, he won both team and individual gold, with all five judges placing him first.

At the age of 18 the big Thoroughbred competed at the 1984 Los Angeles Olympics, placing fourteenth individually. At 19, he was second at the FEI North American Championships, won the West Coast Olympic Selection Trials, and was the US Equestrian Team National Champion for the sixth time.

Keen's Story

Gurney purchased Keen in 1969, when he was three, for $1,000 from a Thoroughbred breeder. The gelding had grown too big to fit in the starting gate! Gurney, who worked her way through college training young horses, had worked with many Thoroughbreds before Keen. "I had sort of developed a system by then," she says. "I did a lot of quiet work and stretching with him to get him to use his back and develop a rhythm. In the beginning I did mostly walk/trot work and didn't canter for quite a while."

Initially she planned to event the big gelding, and she went so far as to compete him at an event at Training Level—which he won. But, he pulled a check ligament in the process. When he was fit again,

Gurney focused on his dressage training, and Keen reached Grand Prix level by age seven. "I wasn't going to jump him anymore then!" Gurney says. She credits longtime US dressage team coach Colonol Bengt Ljungquist with then helping her develop the big horse to his full potential.

Keen was not an easy horse to handle. Gurney says that it took two people, each with a stud chain, to lead him. "He was very, very hot," she explains. But, this energy translated into something special in the arena: the handsome chestnut was a brilliant performer.

Hilda's Advice

People who wish to transition Thoroughbreds "really have to be patient and work on the horse's rhythm," Gurney says. "The rider also has to be careful with the seat and learn to post in a rhythm—using a metronome will help.

"Horses come off the track with no backs," she goes on, "so, using long-and-low work, you have to get them to lengthen the back, not hollow the back." Though Gurney uses side reins in retraining, she cautions, "You want to use them to encourage the horse to stretch, not pull the head in."

Far from working her horse in the ring all the time, Gurney says that she took Keen on many trail rides and still rides her horses out when possible. "Trotting cavalletti is helpful, too," she adds, "and jumping fences with a pole between them teaches the horse to steady and balance itself—an important lesson no matter what you are going to do with the horse."

Courageous Comet
(Comet Shine-Rosinelli)

Rider/Owner: Becky Holder/Tom Holder
Discipline: Eventing

Achievements
Courageous Comet and Becky Holder are on the High Performance Squad of the US Eventing team. In 2005 they were twelfth at the American Eventing Championships Advanced (NC), sixteenth at the Fair Hill CCI*** (MD), and thirty-sixth at the Luhmuhlen CCI**** (GER). The following year they were ninth at The Fork CIC*** (NC) and sixteenth at Rolex Kentucky CCI**** (KY).

Courageous Comet's Story
Holder, who was an alternate for the 2000 Olympic Games with Highland Hogan— another OTTB she trained—purchased "Comet" through Michelle Lawrence in Middleburg, Virginia. As a racehorse he had won $70,000 in 37 starts. At the time of purchase, he walked and trotted under saddle and had popped over some small fences.

"He was a gifted child," says Holder. "I started eventing him in his six-year-old year in

12.2 Becky Holder and Courageous Comet

Florida, and in October of that same year, he did his first one-star event. The next spring he did a two-star at High Park in Colorado. That year, 2003, he also did the three-star at Fair Hill (MD) and was ninth. By 2004, he was on the USET Talent Squad that went to Germany.

"Once he clicked into gear there was no holding back. He's amazing to ride cross-country. Looking through his ears is like looking through a gun sight, he's so focused. He can gallop and then come back with great footwork, so he's very safe cross-country."

Becky's Advice

"Comet was neurotic in the stall, weaving and pacing," she says. "But he loves to be out, so I let him spend a lot of time turned out.

"At home I was not convinced that he would be brave enough to event—he was spooky about terrain, different colored grass, and things like that, though he never had a problem with water or ditches. So, I ponied him off Highland Hogan and he learned to hack out, go over streams and so on. For three months I just took him out and about, no ring work.

"As a rule American Thoroughbreds try hard and put pressure on themselves," Holder says. "I use Gastrogard®, and it makes all the difference in Comet's eating. I notice when he gets nervous or tight, and I change his dose.

"I also had to Initially keep him tied up in his stall at shows because of the PA system," she recalls, "but he's way better now—

he's very personable in his stall. He isn't shy about letting you know what he likes and what he doesn't!"

Relentless Pursuit
(A Lee Rover-Sumptious Gal)

Rider/Owner: Dana Widstrand
Discipline: Eventing

Achievements

Dana Widstrand and Relentless Pursuit won the individual gold medal at the 2003 North American Young Riders' Championships (NAYRC) CCI*, the team gold at the 2006 NAYRC CCI**, and were the top placing Young Rider in the Intermediate Championship at the 2006 Wellpride American Eventing Championships.

Relentless Pursuit's Story

After he raced for one year, "Rover's" breeder reacquired him, and Widstrand—who was 15 years old at the time—purchased him from the breeder. "His old jockey actually jumped him over a couple of barrels," she remembers, "and I rode him a couple of times before I brought him home. Rover was my first horse—I had leased a horse for two years before I bought him. I absolutely just 'got lucky' when I brought him home.

"My trainer came and helped me once a month, and I read a lot and attended a lot

12.3 Dana Widstrand and Relentless Pursuit

of clinics. I also watched and re-watched videos of Rover all the time," Widstrand says. "He lived on a longe line the first couple of months and I still got run off with—luckily it was in a nice big indoor and he couldn't go too far."

The pair competed at the Preliminary Level in 2002 and 2003 and qualified for the North American Young Rider Championships, where they actually had their first clear cross-country round and won the CCI*. After that they moved up to Intermediate Level, but Widstrand says that she was a "stubborn teenager" and had a lot of trouble.

In 2004 Widstrand took Rover with her to work full time for event trainer Mark

Weissbecker, who helped her get her training back on track. She had a successful competition year at the Intermediate Level in 2006, and today the pair is working on moving up to the Advanced Level.

Widstrand says she still catches a glimpse of Rover's previous life at the track every now and then. "When we gallop he has to be at the front of the group—he'll grab the bit and take you to the front. Even when we ride with my boyfriend on his bike, Rover always wants to get ahead of the bike."

Dana's Advice
"The best thing I've done for my horse is turn him out," Widstrand says. "He lives in a herd with a run-in shed, and that has been a huge deal for him—it's helped his brain a lot. Also, he loves his job. I think Thoroughbreds need to find their niche and then they're great."

Widstrand encourages everyone to get professional help in order to avoid neglecting aspects of the horse's training. "The hardest part that gave me the most stress," she recalls, "was when I came to Mark [Weissbecker] and he said, 'So, you have no basics on the flat, huh?' We had to go relearn the basics and establish leg and seat to hand and getting Rover 'uncurled.' There was a huge hole in his training."

"I think I got lucky," Widstrand adds, touching upon the fact that Rover was very young when she purchased him. "There are some babies out there that could not handle what Rover put up with. Something with more mileage would really be better for an inexperienced rider.

"It did mature my riding, though," she admits with a smile. "I had to really learn how to stay on!"

Bingo Helen
(2000 Crimson Guard-Royal Wiz)

Rider/Owner: Lisa Croxton
Discipline: Dressage

Achievements
Croxton and Bingo Helen won the Southeast Virginia Dressage Association 2006 End of the Year Reserve Champion title at Training Level and were third at First Level.

Bingo Helen's Story
"Bingo" raced only two times with earnings of $530. Deemed "not competitive," she was retired sound and turned out for at least a year before she was donated to New Vocations. She was with the program only two weeks when Croxton adopted her.

With the help of her trainer Kathy Rowse, who rode Bingo Helen once a week, Croxton worked on adding weight and muscle tone, and improving Bingo's movement, which tended to be short and tense. For the first few months they worked on moving long and low and stretching Bingo's muscles through her back.

While she was comfortable to ride at walk and trot, the canter was harder and took longer to improve. "She jumped up and down instead of forward with her hind legs," Rowse explains. "Canter transitions were so tight that sometimes she bucked or exploded. Lisa [Croxton] always concentrated on her basics and persevered as she worked on being quiet with her seat and her aids."

As Bingo's muscling changed she began to perform better, connecting from back to front and using her hind legs. Croxton used lateral work and transitions within the gaits to get her more active and responsive, making sure that she was clear and precise with her aids and always getting a reaction from Bingo but not pushing her too quick in her tempo.

"Although it seems to take forever to cement the basics," says Rowse, "horses always seem to move quickly after that."

Croxton began showing Bingo and at the end of their first year, and they are now schooling Second Level dressage. "We are focusing on more recognized shows in 2007 for our USDF Rider Performance Awards for Training and First Level," says Croxton. "My goal is to work for our USDF Bronze Medal in 2008–2009."

"This is truly a success story," insists Rowse. "I think it is a combination of Lisa's horsemanship and her belief in Bingo as well as Bingo's desire to please. Lisa is truly a dedicated rider and spends much time taking care of her horse, and Bingo is certainly happy to have such a loving 'mother' who cares for her every need. The result is a muscled, sleek, shiny dressage horse who has very good basics and is just waiting to move up the levels."

Lisa's Advice

Croxton grew up riding and showing mostly Quarter Horses, and she observed marked differences in the way Thoroughbreds need to be handled.

"The one thing I have learned about Thoroughbreds is that they need a lot of time and patience," she says. "They are sensitive horses and can be nervous. Our major key for transitional training was a lot of patience and constancy. My trainer helped encourage me and built our confidence." Croxton also recommends lots of groundwork and longeing in the early stages of retraining.

Care and management played a big role in Bingo's development, as conscientious attention to her weight and muscle helped improve her movement. "I also want to thank [farrier] George Brehm for all his patience and quality work," Croxton adds. "Bingo needed a lot of work on her hooves, because they were flared and cracked."

Croxton feels that Thoroughbreds are a particularly special breed. "Build a trusting bond, and they will do most anything you ask of them," she says. "I always get tickled when I go to catch Bingo Helen from her field, and she is happy to see me and nickers to greet me. She won't let anyone else catch her, only me. We are a team now and we will be working together for many years to come. Bingo is my best friend."

Fair Grape
(Fair Skies-Gray Grape)

Rider/Owner: Christy Baxter
Discipline: Hunters

Achievements

Christy Baxter and Fair Grape (now shown as "After the Rain") have won numerous championships in various hunter divisions.

Fair Grape's Story

After a short, undistinguished career—finishing only three of five races at Beulah Park and Thistledowns Raceway—"Rain's" earnings amounted to $2,352. He was retired due to breathing problems, and sent to New Vocations directly from the track. Baxter adopted him three weeks later.

Rain was said to be a "double-sided roarer," a very uncommon situation where both arytenoid cartilages in the larynx were para-

12.5 Christy Baxter and Fair Grape

lyzed, and he had great difficulty breathing. Rain was very lethargic and tried to exert as little energy as possible in everything he did.

Baxter had tieback surgery performed, "re-opening" the larynx, and it was very successful—she found that there was a huge dif-ference in Rain once he could breath more easily. He started to act like a three-year- old again, running around and playing like a nor-mal horse.

Rain was underweight, so Baxter had to increase his weight as she built up his breathing tolerance. After about six months, he could do an hour of work and no longer had problems breathing. With the help of her trainer, Baxter worked on Rain's flatwork and basic strengthening skills during this time.

Building Rain up to compete as a hunter was a long process. When he turned four years old, Baxter faced the challenge of teaching the long-legged 17-hand gelding to jump. He was not sure what to do with his legs at first—he was very clumsy and unbalanced. However, with patience and time he became a beautiful jumper and very competitive in the hunter ring. Christy now shows him in the 3'3" Adult Amateur hunters. He has been named Champion many times at various shows and has shown successfully at the Winter Equestrian Festival in Wellington, Florida.

"Rain is a huge success story," says Baxter. "Many said he would never be able to do anything because of his breathing, but he proved everybody wrong. He will always have a home with me. Rain is like my child, and I thank God every day for bringing him into my life"

Christy's Advice
"I believe the main key to transitioning a Thoroughbred is giving him the time to learn to become a horse," says Baxter. "Most of them have no idea what it is like to be turned out, have time spent on their grooming, or even receive love and attention from a single person. Giving an OTTB time to relax and 'get their brains right,' with turnout and care, is so important."

Rain is a testimony to this theory—Baxter and her trainer gave him about a month or so off to transition to "just being a horse." "He was turned out a lot," Baxter says, "and we did a lot of groundwork with him. We worked with him every day, slowly teaching him how to be a hunter."

Rollin Onoverdrive
(Rollin On Over-Tiffany Drive)

Owner/Rider: Mary Jo Gehrum
Discipline: Trail Riding

Achievements
Mary Jo Gehrum is not stingy with her praise of "Driver." "He is now truly trustworthy on the trail," she says, "and I am finally able to relax and enjoy the scenery. When we get in dangerous or tricky situations (we ride in some pretty remote areas), Driver knows to stop, look at the obstacle in front of him, and pick the best way through without injuring himself or me.

"We have ridden as many as 40 miles in a day, and Driver has learned to pace himself because it's going to be a long one. He is a very brave horse—nothing spooks him and he is always willing to try something new. He has now graduated to being a 'mature' trail horse capable of showing our recently adopted Standardbred the ropes of trail riding."

12.6 Mary Jo Gehrum and Rollin Onoverdrive

Rollin Onoverdrive's Story

Driver had 61 starts, six wins, and won $48,153 from three to nine years of age. "As you can tell by his race history," says Gehrum, "Driver was pretty set in his track ways when I adopted him. I'm sure his transition was much harder than it would be for a horse that had only raced for a year or two."

Because of the length of time Driver spent at the track, Gehrum faced several significant challenges in his retraining. He had some bad track habits, such as weaving and spinning in his stall (solved by turning him out as much as possible), and he was hard to keep weight on. "Food is not one of his high priorities," Gehrum says. "He allows any little distraction to pull him away from eating." This short attention span was also a problem when riding him. When he had had enough for the day, "he would fidget and dance and pretty much act like a spoiled child."

Teaching him to trot under saddle was

another issue early on. "He didn't even realize that he knew how to trot," Gehrum recalls. "It was either walk or rocket into a gallop." Driver paid little attention to his surroundings, and rather than watch where he was going, he would simply race down the trail, full speed ahead. "We would step in very deep mud, almost bump into trees head on, get dangerously close to cliff edges—all because he was sure that the idea was to get there fast and first."

So what did it take to finally make a successful transition from track to trail? "Time under saddle, miles of trails, patience, repetition, and never expecting more than the horse was capable of giving," says Gehrum. "I truly love and appreciate Driver now. He gives me horse hugs and loves when I kiss his face. Transitioning Driver has created a very strong bond between us that I can't imagine would have developed if we hadn't faced so many challenges together.

"There is nothing like traveling down an open trail on a fit Thoroughbred who can not only provide as much speed as I ask for, but then immediately slows when I sink my weight back into the saddle. Climbing hills or even mini-mountains are never a problem for him—Driver always reaches deep inside of himself and meets the challenge. I'm sure that reaction is also one of his track habits (and in this case not a bad one). His Thoroughbred heart enables him to always find more 'go.'"

Mary Jo's Advice

"Having an experienced trail horse to act as a teacher is invaluable," says Gehrum. "My husband and his mature trail horse Rambo helped me transition Driver from racing Thoroughbred to dependable trail mount. There were a couple of times in the first six months that Jim had to pull Rambo in front of us on the trail in order to get Driver to slow down!"

Most importantly, Gehrum says you need to "be patient and show the horse lots of love; be persistent and don't expect overnight results."

Triomphe Spitfire
(Secretito-Triomphe)

Rider/Owner: Bailey Farrell
Discipline: Pony Club

Achievements

"Tucker" has taken Bailey Farrell to her "C-1" rating in Pony Club, confidently jumping 4'3" with the potential to go higher.

Triomphe Spitfire's Story

Originally purchased as a weanling for $20,000 at Keeneland Sales, Tucker raced eight times, earning only $1,328. He came to New Vocations and was adopted by Farrell when she was 13 years old. Though Farrell was very young, her mother had an ex-

12.7 Bailey Farrell and Triomphe Spitfire

racehorse of her own, and Tucker was a very quiet, relaxed individual.

The day after they brought him home, he jumped the pasture fence and cleared it. "A week after we got him, in early February, I took him on a ride with my mom on her ex-racehorse, Robbie," says Farrell. "My mom's horse would not go through the frozen creek at the start of the trail, but Tucker marched right through."

Farrell decided that Tucker had the talent and bravery to be an eventer, but for the first two months, she just did trail riding and light ring work. "I think that the trails worked wonders for him," she says now, "as he has never been afraid of any obstacle on a cross-country course."

Progressively, the pair began work over ground poles, then small cross-rails with placing poles (ground poles 6 to 7 feet out from the jump, to ensure that the horse enters with good striding). "I never once pushed him beyond his comfort zone, and made sure that I gave him positive experiences, over and over again," says Farrell.

For the next year Tucker jumped low fences in increasingly complicated combinations, and Tucker competed in his first Beginner Novice event at the Kentucky Horse Park. She continued showing him that summer, giving him lots of exposure.

"One day, my mom said to me 'Bailey, I think your horse is bored with 2-foot fences,'" remembers Farrell. "So, I reluctantly raised the fences, and Tucker's eyes lit up! It was as if he said, 'Finally, you are putting my potential to the test!' All of our low, progressive confidence builders had paid off, and now Tucker confidently jumps 4'3"—and I can tell it is nowhere near his limit.

"Tucker and I have a very special bond that keeps us going and very happy. For this, I am eternally grateful."

Bailey's Advice

"The most important thing is patience," says Farrell. "Instead of getting frustrated over something, I would go back to basics and just trail ride for the rest of the day. Another thing is to be sure you know what a behavior means before reacting to it. I always would seek advice before punishing misbehavior, in case it was caused by confusion and not a bad attitude.

"Don't give up! Any horse needs a transitioning period to become accustomed to a new life, but if you just stick it out, most likely it will work out. Also, remember how *different* this new life is for racehorses. They have only been exposed to the racing world and need to understand what you want before they can do it."

Entirety
(Easy Gallop-Take Advantage)

Owner/Rider: Jane and John Gallagher
Discipline: Foxhunting

Achievements

Entirety ("General") became Jane Gallagher's favorite field hunter. He foxhunted first flight, front of the pack until age 29, then retired to trail riding and hunting occasionally second flight, back of the pack. When her husband John, an inexperienced rider, wanted to take up foxhunting, General took care of him. He proved gentle with children and often carries the couple's two young daughters around the farm.

Entirety's Story

General had raced for five years when Gallagher bought him off the track as a seven-year-old. "I've seen a lot of horses come off the track and a lot of them took a lot longer, but with him it just fell into place," she says.

One part of his training that she did have to work on was galloping in a group of horses without racing. Gallagher arranged training sessions where two friends on horseback would ride with her, one on each side. Then, they would trot, canter, or gallop forward while Gallagher made General wait.

In the hunt field he was always a strong horse. "At first he was a little unruly," admits Gallagher. "But I've jumped him over 4'—he's very bold and brave.

"Once I took him out on the trail and ended up on a big mountain, with a ferocious storm rolling in," she recalls. "Then a buck appeared in the woods. He was about nine years old then and so courageous—he handled everything perfectly, including going back down the mountain, which was so steep he had to slide down! He was always just great—if you pointed him in the right direction and got his speed going he would stay the course, as long as you could hang on."

Jane's Advice

Find a way to make your horse happy.

"I couldn't turn General out alone," says Gallagher. "So I turned him out with a herd so that he could be the boss. And, he doesn't like to get cold—you can just tell when he's miserable. We make sure that he can always get in and out of the weather."

And General didn't like standing on the trailer, though once the rig was moving, he traveled fine. So Gallagher always loaded him at the last minute and started driving right away.

Says Gallagher, with a smile, "We treat him like royalty, so he acts like royalty."

12.8 Jane Gallagher and Entirety (right)

Resources

OTTB Adoption Programs

Angel Acres Horse Haven Rescue (PA) www.angelacreshorsehavenrescue.com

B.I.T.S. (KS) www.bitshorseadopt.org

ReRun, Inc. (KY, NJ, NY, MA, PA) www.Rerun.org

Bright Futures Farm (PA) www.brightfuturesfarm.org

California Equine Retirement Foundation (CA) www.cerfhorses.org

CANTER (MI, OH, PA, IL, New England, Mid-Atlantic) www.canterusa.org

Days End Farm Horse Rescue (MD) www.defhr.org

Equine Rescue & Rehabilitation, Inc. (MD) www.horserescue.com

Exceller Fund (CA) www.excellerfund.org

Finger Lakes Thoroughbred Adoption Program (NY) www.fingerlakestap.org

Glen Ellen Vocational Academy (CA) www.glenellenfarms.com/geva

Horse Lovers United, Inc. (MD) www.horseloversunited.com

Horse Net, Inc. (MD) www.horsenethorserescue.org

LaMancha Animal Rescue (PA) www.LaManchaAnimalRescue.org

Lost & Found Horse Rescue (PA) www.lostandfoundhorserescue.com

MidAtlantic Horse Rescue (MD) www.midatlantichorserescue.org

New Vocations Racehorse Adoption Program (OH, MI, TN) www.horseadoption.com

New York Horse Rescue Corporation (NY) www.nyhr.org

Secretariat Center (KY) www.thoroughbredadoptions.com

Thoroughbred Retirement Foundation (NY) www.trfinc.org

Tranquility Farm (CA) www.tranquilityfarmtbs.org

United Pegasus Foundation (CA) www.unitedpegasus.com

Whimsical Animal Rescue/Large Animal Division (DE) www.whimsicalequine.rescuegroups.org

Recommended Reading and Viewing

101 Longeing & Long Lining Exercises—English & Western: A Ringside Guide by Cherry Hill,
www.wiley.com/WileyCDA/Section/id-101743.html

All Horse Systems Go: The Horse Owner's Full-Color Veterinary and Conditioning Reference for Modern Performance, Sport, and Pleasure Horses by Nancy S. Loving, DVM,
www.horseandriderbooks.com

Back to Work: How to Rehabilitate or Recondition Your Horse by Lucinda Dyer,
www.horseandriderbooks.com

The Bit and the Reins: Developing Good Contact and Sensitive Hands by Gerhard Kapitzke,
www.horseandriderbooks.com

The Horse's Pain-Free Back and Saddle-Fit Book: Ensure Soundness and Comfort with Back Analysis and Correct use of Saddles and Pads by Joyce Harman, DVM, MRCVS,
www.horseandriderbooks.com

On the Muscle: Portrait of a Thoroughbred Racing Stable, Pony Highway Productions,
www.ponyhighway.com

Understanding Equine Lameness by Les Sellnow, www.eclipsepress.com

Understanding Equine Nutrition by Karen Briggs, www.eclipsepress.com

Recommended Web Sites

www.equine.com

www.equineline.com

www.equineprotectionnetwork.com

www.dreamhorse.com

www.horse-protection.org

www.jockeyclub.com

www.unwantedhorsecoalition.org

Acknowledgments

I would like to recognize and thank God for creating a truly magnificent animal when he made the Thoroughbred. I feel very blessed to have the opportunity to work with God's creation each day. It is because of his presence in my life that I am able to do what I do.

Without the help of many people, this book would not have been possible. It has been a team effort from the beginning, and I would like to thank everyone who has played a part, large or small. To my whole family, the New Vocations staff, and co-writer Amber Heintzberger: Thanks for your time, support, and valued input. To the Thoroughbred trainers and owners, photographers, adopters, New Vocations horses, and program donors: It has been an ever-challenging, but fun and rewarding ride, and I am truly thankful for all of your support and help along the way. It is my hope that through our efforts more people will take in an off-the-track Thoroughbred and give him a chance at a new life.

There are several people I would like to thank by name. First and foremost, I would like to express my gratitude to my husband Kenneth. I thank God every day for blessing me with such an amazing and supportive husband. There were many long days and nights, and he was always there to give encouragement and bring me coffee. Thank you for putting up with all the long hours.

My parents, Charley and Dot Morgan, not only taught me most of what I know about horses and the racing industry, but more importantly, they instilled in me their pure and honest morals and values. They have always been a light in this world, and I can only hope to be the same.

If it were not for my mother, New Vocations would not exist. It was her passion and vision that started something special in 1992, and the organization has now grown into the largest racehorse adoption program in the US. Not only am I grateful for her efforts, but over 2,000 OTTBs and their adoptive owners are, as well.

My older sister Winnie has been a big influence in my life. She has always been the most loyal friend, and I continue to look up to her.

Many thanks to the staff at New Vocations. Words cannot express how great it is to work on a daily basis with a team of people who truly want to make a difference in the racing industry. Each member plays a significant role in our mission and all are equally needed. It is because of this devoted group that over 300 retired racehorses are now successfully placed into new homes each year.

Lastly, I would like to thank you, the reader, for seeing the importance in giving an OTTB a new career. Anyone who is willing to take a little time and face a rewarding challenge can help one of these special horses transition to a new life.

Index